D0087613

Crossing Boundaries

Crossing Boundaries

Selected Writings

Albert O. Hirschman

ZONE BOOKS · NEW YORK

1998

© 1998 Albert O. Hirschman
Zone Books
611 Broadway, Suite 608
New York, NY 10012

"Trespassing: Places and Ideas in the Course of a Life"
originally published in Italy as *Passaggi di Frontiera: I luoghi e
le idee di un percorso di vita* © 1994 Donzelli Editore.

Printed in the United States of America.

Distributed by The MIT Press,
Cambridge, Massachusetts, and London, England

Library of Congress Cataloging-in-Publication Data

Hirschman, Albert O.
     Crossing boundaries: selected writings/Albert O.
  Hirschman.
     p. cm.
     Includes bibliographical references (p.   ).
     ISBN 1-890951-04-8
     1. Marshall Plan. 2. Economic assistance — Europe.
     3. Economic assistance — Latin America.
     4. Democracy. 5. Social sciences. I. Title.
HC240.H544   1998
338.91'7304 – dc21   97-47702
                                                CIP

Contents

Preface

The first chapter of this book, which I originally delivered as the Jan Patocka Memorial Lecture at the Institute for Human Sciences in Vienna in 1996, discusses the interface between the public and the private and deals in particular with the connection between the common meal in Greece and the "invention" of democracy in Athens.

The second chapter was written on the occasion of the fiftieth anniversary of the Marshall Plan, for a conference in June 1997 at Harvard University. A special effort was made here to connect my personal experience under the Marshall Plan with my decision to pursue a wholly different career — as an economic adviser in Latin America.

The third chapter of this book is a lengthy interview I gave jointly to Carmine Donzelli, Marta Petrusewicz, and Claudia Rusconi in 1993. This interview was conducted in Italian. It was published in 1994 as a small book by Carmine Donzelli, who had by then established himself as an editor in Rome. Subsequent versions of the Italian edition appeared in German, Spanish, and French.[1] In 1997, I at last translated the Italian into English. At the same time, I corrected and considerably edited the text.

A collection of essays I published some years ago (in 1981)

was entitled *Essays in Trespassing*. As I explained in the 1981 preface to that book, what unified the articles included there was their tendency to "cross boundaries from one social science domain to another." When Carmine Donzelli published the interview I gave him and his colleagues in 1993, he entitled the volume *Passaggi di frontiera*. As I translated these words into English, I was carried back to the notion of "crossing" which I decided to adopt as the title of the present book. Crossing boundaries is not only characteristic of the physical moves I have undertaken (or had to undertake) in the course of my life; it is also distinctive of the interdisciplinary travels I have engaged in ever since I started to write.

By the time of the interview I gave to Carmine Donzelli and his collaborators in 1993, I had reconsidered my long-standing neglect of the autobiographical genre. In the face of ever more insistent demands, and considering also my advancing age, I decided voluntarily to engage in memory building. Moreover, the composition of the "Donzelli Committee" ensured that I would be asked questions that touched on both the adventurous and the speculative sides of my life. Thus, the first two parts of the interview, "The European Years" and "The American Years," are concerned primarily with my various migrations, while the final part, entitled "Key Terms," engages a variety of concepts and ideas that have shaped my life.

In sum, the first chapters of the book, on commensality and the Marshall Plan, have much in common with the last part of the interview, that is, the "key-concepts" of my life.

Albert O. Hirschman
Princeton, New Jersey
December, 1997

8

NOTE

1. The German translation, by Sophie Alf, appeared in 1995 in the journal *Leviathan*, vol. 23, sec. 2, pp. 263–304. The Spanish translation appeared in the Argentinean journal *Desarrollo Economico*, vol. 35, Jan.–Mar. 1996, pp. 629–64. The translators into Spanish were Mercedes Botto and Agustín Rojo. The French translation appeared in 1997 in a separate publication of mine entitled *La Morale secrète de l'économiste* by Les Belles Lettres, Paris. The French translator was Pierre-Emmanuel Dauzat.

CHAPTER ONE

Melding the Public and

Private Spheres:

Taking Commensality Seriously

I have argued recently that "at some point in one's life, self-subversion may become the principal means to self-renewal" (Hirschman 1995, 92). I hope to subvert here a book I published in 1982, *Shifting Involvements: Private Interest and Public Action*. It explored the reasons modern societies may be "predisposed toward oscillation between periods of intense preoccupation with public issues and of almost total concentration on individual improvement and private welfare goals." Many of the reasons I gave for such periodic shifts seem to me to be valid still. But I want to go back to one particular phase of the alleged "private/public cycle," which I now view in a different light.

The principal motive force that drove my story was *disappointment*. Disappointment with the concentration on private consumption was for me a primary source of the subsequent turn toward action in the public interest, just as in the following phase disappointment with the turn toward action in the public interest would promote the return to private concerns. It so happened that during the post-World War II period with which I started my account, private consumption in the Western economies rose primarily in the area of durable goods — automobiles, refrigerators, washing machines, televisions, and so on. This "drive to high mass consumption" was celebrated by Walt W. Rostow in his highly successful work, *Stages of Economic Growth* (1960). I wrote my book some twenty years later, with the benefit of hindsight, that is, *after* the world had passed through the violent student agitation and unrest of the late 1960s, which were widely interpreted as a protest against the latest Rostovian stage. By then that stage had come to be known as "consumerism," a term that was often used in a derogatory vein.

Had Rostow been overenthusiastic about the massive expansion in consumer durables that had indeed marked the postwar prosperity in the United States, and had rapidly spread to Western Europe, Japan, and elsewhere? Had he failed to see some dangerous portents in this expansion?

Such was the opinion of a stimulating book that, without actually mentioning Rostow's positive account of the consumer durables boom, offered a new and highly original analysis of consumer satisfaction and dissatisfaction. I am referring to Tibor Scitovsky's *The Joyless Economy* (1976), which was written in the aftermath of the student revolts and influenced me strongly.

Right at the beginning of his book, Scitovsky refers starkly to its historical background: the downfall of American consumers from the brief (Rostovian) triumph they had celebrated at the middle of the twentieth century, when they spent "the world's highest income on the world's most copied and coveted life-style." Within a decade, this self-image was to be largely destroyed, and Scitovsky asks: "Could it be that we seek our satisfaction in the wrong things, or in the wrong way, and are then dissatisfied with the outcome?" (Scitovsky 1976, 2–4). This question, of course, contradicted the traditional economic approach, according to which consumers know what is good for them and calculate expertly how to maximize their satisfactions. But Scitovsky protested against this simplistic and apologetic tradition and devoted his first chapters to various complications and illuminating explorations in individual psychology.

For me the most interesting distinction he developed was that between comfort and pleasure. The human drives to relieve discomfort and to achieve comfort do make for pleasure in two ways. First of all, pleasure is generated by repeated travel from varieties of discomfort to *comfort* (e.g., from hunger to satiation). Second, pleasure occurs also as we move from inactivity or boredom to renewed activity, as a result of various types of *stimulation*. To the extent that countries become economically advanced and affluent, the first ingredient of pleasure — the journey from discomfort to comfort — is reduced or held at bay; hence stimulation should take over as a major source of pleasure. But with people being hardly conscious of the contrast between pleasure and comfort, they pursue the latter at the expense of stimulation and suffer a deficiency in overall pleasure. Thus they end up in Scitovsky's "joyless economy."

This description of the Scitovsky model leaves out many of its finer features; but even in this stripped-down form, it becomes clear how it enabled me to produce my own story of successive disappointments. Paradoxically, I made this story start out with the *expansion* of private consumption of durable goods, an expansion that, just a short while ago, had been considered the essence of various "economic miracles."

My main point was wholly inspired by Scitovsky. In comparison with conventional purchases, new durable goods were more weighted with comfort than with pleasure. As a result, the first massive appearance of durables in a consumer culture will produce an "initially disconcerting" change in the traditional balance of pleasure and comfort (Hirschman 1981, 33). I did mention some obvious qualifications: the generation that first experiences the new comfort/pleasure balance will no doubt be delighted with its new acquisitions and deeply grateful for the emancipation from work and fatigue it has achieved. But gratitude never lasts very long. As the new durables are increasingly taken for granted, the extra comfort and time they provide must be taken advantage of and be occupied by new forms of stimulation. In the absence of such stimulation, disappointment will set in. A large part of Scitovsky's book is devoted to these topics.

My principal argument against Scitovsky was his utter neglect of the *public* dimension. He did not conceive of politics, participation in public life, pursuit of the public interest (or of "public happiness," in the language of the eighteenth century) as alternative sources of stimulation. I still believe it is worthwhile to explore such alternatives to a predominantly private life. But my original critique along these lines remained imprisoned in the two mutually exclusive categories of the private and the public. I failed to realize that there are important occasions when the public and the private meld and merge.

In doing so I was perhaps merely following an ancient tradition. Take, for example, the biological function of filling one's stomach. This has long been considered a purely private activity that was contrasted with the pursuit of "higher," spiritual values and was often treated with disdain in comparison.

The Bible, Pascal, and Samuelson

Both the Old and the New Testaments laid down the rule that "man does not live by bread alone" (Deuteronomy 8:3; Matthew 4:4), and that it was far more important to follow the Lord's commands than to eat. These two activities were eventually taken to stand in opposition to one another, and during the later Middle Ages fasting became the essence of meritorious religious behavior. As Caroline Bynum pointed out in *Holy Feast and Holy Fast*, this was especially true for women: Raymond of Capua, the biographer of Saint Catherine of Siena, felt much guilt about his own difficulties in fasting and found Catherine to be a true model in this regard.[1]

During the Renaissance, the pleasures of eating and the excitement over food and drink staged a vigorous comeback, a development exemplified by Rabelais and his characters Gargantua and Pantagruel. In contrast to the myth of the lost paradise, Rabelais knows of no punishment for gluttony or other cardinal sins. He celebrates even drink as that "ambrosial, delicious, precious, celestial, joyous and deific" liquor.[2] But his amoral and guiltless attitude toward food and drink did not last long. Already Montaigne qualified the endorsement of food by saying, "one must look out not so much at what one eats as with whom one eats" and he further downgraded the delights of eating by adding: "There is no dish so sweet to me, and no sauce so appetizing as the pleasure derived from society" (Montaigne 1933, bk. 3, 13). As was to be pointed out much later by Georg Simmel, the social delights Montaigne talks about here are to be had primarily as a result of, and in conjunction with, the common meal and should therefore not be contrasted with it. But the intellectual tradition stemming from the Bible had long separated the consumption of food from the so-called higher activities. This separation was soon to be fully restored by Pascal.

In one of his longer *Pensées*, Pascal distinguishes two different ways of pursuing happiness and justice: One consists in following the commands of God, the other in acquiring instead a great variety of objects meant to take the place of God. Here Pascal compiles a long, intentionally incongruous list of objects: "stars, sky, land, elements, plants, cabbage, leeks, animals, insects, calves, snakes, fever, plague, war, famine, vices, adultery, incest." Then he continues:

Since man has lost the true Good, all of these things will seem to be like the Good, including even man's self-destruction which is so contrary to God, to reason and to nature...but those who have come close [to the truth] have concluded that the universal Good which all men desire...should not consist in any of the particular things which can be possessed only by an individual—but that this Good must be such that *all can possess it at the same time*, without diminution or envy, and that nobody can lose it against his own will. (Pascal 1969, 1185–86, emphasis added.)

Pascal then contrasts the belief in God, available to all those who believe in Him, with the partaking in tangible commodities, such as cabbage and leeks, which are necessarily appropriated and, in these cases, eaten by individual consumers. Economists will find Pascal's contrast surprisingly close to the distinction they are used to making between public and private goods (or bads).[3] Following Paul Samuelson's classic formulation in the 1950s, private goods have been defined as those that are held and consumed individually, while public goods are those whose consumption and enjoyment by one citizen does not affect the quantity available to others (Samuelson 1954 and 1955). Interestingly enough, the good that occurred to Samuelson to stand as a typical example of private goods was the loaf of bread ("whose total can be parceled out among two or more persons, with one man having a loaf less if another gets a loaf more" [Samuelson 1955, 350]), while the typical public goods were such "non-rival" services as police protection, national defense, and public education.

When this distinction was first clearly made, in the immediate postwar period, public opinion about the role of the state was on the whole quite positive and public goods were celebrated, in spite of the intrinsic difficulties of estimating the demand for them. A well-known article written in the 1960s by Robert Dorfman reflected this attitude:

> Since [nobody] can be precluded from enjoying [public goods], it is in the interest of each [person] to avoid contributing to them if he can. Therefore the coercive power of the state must be enlisted to compel contributions. And when this is done *wisely* all benefit, for the goods desired by all (or virtually all) can be provided which would otherwise be unavailable to any. Goods of this nature, then, can be provided only by the state, by philanthropists, and as by-products of certain private goods. (Dorfman 1969, 249, emphasis added.)

This passage looks at the distinction between public and private goods very much as the Bible had done. Bread was to be eaten by the individual consumer; but providing it "alone," by itself, was far from enough: to assure the good life for all citizens, various *public* goods must be concurrently produced by the state.

The economist's distinction between private and public goods thus retained and reinforced the basic dichotomy of the Bible and of Pascal. Little attention was paid to goods that would somehow be intermediate between the private and the public category or would belong to both.

Georg Simmel

In the meantime, however, a distinguished sociologist had called attention to situations where goods that *seem* to be wholly private actually have important collective dimensions. In a short but penetrating article written in 1910, *Die Soziolgie der Mahlzeit*, Simmel refers in this connection to the social institution of the meal. Almost at the beginning of the paper, a striking paragraph points to the function of the meal as a bridge between the private and public functions of food and drink when consumed in common by a group:

> Let us take what is most common to men and women among all the things they have in common: the fact that they must eat and drink. This is precisely what is most self-centered about them, most unconditional, direct, and limited to the individual: What I think, I can let others know about; what I see, I can show to others; what I say can be heard by hundreds of others — but what is eaten by a single person can under no circumstances be eaten by anyone else. In none of the higher realms is it ever the case that what should be had by one person must be unconditionally renounced by others. But since this primitive physiological fact is an absolutely general human characteristic, it becomes precisely a communal action: thus arises the sociological construct of the meal — it turns the exclusive self-seeking of eating into the frequent experience of being together and into the habit of joining in a common purpose — something that is but rarely achieved by occasions of a higher, more spiritual order. Persons who do not share any interest can join in the common meal — in this possibility, mediated through the primitive and transparent character of material interest, *lies the immense sociological significance of the meal.*[4]

This basic point is then worked out by Simmel through the principal characteristics of the meal. The German language is helpful to Simmel's enterprise as *Mahlzeit*, the German word for meal, already refers, through the inclusion of the term *Zeit* (time), to some of the *social* features of the occasion. *Mahlzeit* denotes the regularity and simultaneity of the meal, or what is also known as its "commensality." A more common term today is *conviviality*, but I shall use here the more technical term — which derives from *mensa* (table) — for eating together around a table.

18

Commensality includes friends and family, but excludes irreconcilable enemies. According to a French author, it brings with it the *douceur* of having been included as well as the cruelty of being excluded (Morineau 1987). In German, moreover, the term *Mahlzeit* has long been used also as an exclamation celebrating commensality at the beginning of the joint meal, as a term of benediction when a group sits down together to eat. The exclamation served as an abbreviation for the more religious invocation *"Gesegnete Mahlzeit!"* (May this meal be blessed).

Simmel's basic insight about the meal providing a connection between two very different spheres — those of the selfish individual and of the social collective — leads him to throw light on various other ways in which eating has been "civilized," from the rules that were set for eating from the pot and later from plates, to the use and manner of holding knife, fork, and spoon, and even to the appropriate decoration of the dining room. It is odd that Norbert Elias should not have referred to the Simmel essay in his *The Civilizing Process* (1981), in spite of the fact that his famous work is obviously written with similar questions in mind (Elias's book was once reviewed under the title "The Rise of the Fork"). But Elias wrote as an historical sociologist and was interested in the details of changing institutions and habits, whereas Simmel wrote as a social theorist and developed his ideas purely as deductions from general principles. Even the shape of the plate is thus deduced! Simmel derives its circular shape with a uniform radius from the principle that an identical portion of food is normally meant to be distributed to each participant in the meal and exclaims: "The plates of a table do not tolerate any individuality."

Toward the end of his essay, Simmel characteristically moves in an unexpected direction. His story rises first from the natural-physical to the social-aesthetic. But in a final twist, Simmel interrupts or qualifies this ascent by noting that the basic need to eat does not permit a wholly free flow of conversation. Thus he defends the "banality of normal table talk" and sets a definite ceiling to the lofty and possibly controversial sphere to which the meal was almost about to take us.

Simmel's essay confirmed the positive light under which I had presented, in *Shifting Involvements*, the "truly nondurable" goods — that is, those that, like food and fuel, are actually *used up* in the process of consumption. Influenced by Scitovsky's distinction between comfort and pleasure, I had thought that these goods would cause less disappointment than durables: food vanishes in the course of consumption and therefore permits the process of pleasure generation to start over again — with the next mouthful, once the travel from discomfort to comfort is resumed. But it now seems likely to me that in celebrating these "truly nondurable" goods, I followed a correct instinct, but invoked inadequate reasons: I continued to look at eating and food intake as purely private and self-centered activities. Like Scitovsky and most economists, I neglected their potential public dimension.

The superiority of food over what I called "possessions" is primarily rooted in Simmel's insight about the meal: it is the ease with which the private consumption of food is connected with collective or public endeavors, due to commensality. Implicitly, Simmel compares eating with other basic physiological drives, such as sleeping, and he finds that among them only the intake of food is performed in common and therefore will lead to "essential communal actions": it is the "frequent experience of being together" and the "habit of joining in a common purpose" which make for the "immense sociological importance of the meal."

It appears that in disregarding the Simmelian shift from the private to the public domain through the common meal, we have failed to recognize the substantial *external benefits* of this type of food consumption. Economists — Scitovsky figures importantly among them — often feel that the discovery of external benefits justifies the payment of subsidies to the activity responsible for such benefits. For example, the existence of external benefits is often cited as an argument for the provision of public subsidies to the arts (Throsby 1994; Baumol 1995). I have no intention of making a plea here for subsidies to public meals, in part because the external benefits can turn into losses, as will be noted toward the end of this essay. But it is instructive to point out that subsidies to common meals or banquets did in fact exist and played a considerable role at one time in history — in ancient Greece, to cite one well-documented example.

The Banquet and Democracy
The venerable existence and importance of the Greek banquet with its religious sacrifices has long been known. It was already described in brief but glowing terms over a century ago by Fustel de Coulanges in *La Cité antique* (1864) and by Jakob Burckhardt in his *Griechische Kulturgeschichte* (1898). The topic has continued to be much studied by historians, iconographers, and epigraphers of the ancient Greek world, and during recent years these studies (of writings, vases, and inscriptions) have greatly expanded. A comprehensive treatise was published recently by the Hellenist Pauline Schmitt Pantel, under the title *La Cité au banquet: Histoire des repas publics dans les cités grecques* (1992; subsequent parenthetical citations refer to this book). This rich work presents the evolution, over a period of almost ten centuries, of the banquet among the Greeks.

Usually, archaic Greece is distinguished from the classical, principally Athenian period of the fifth and fourth century B.C., which is, in turn, marked off from the Hellenistic era. During the archaic period, Schmitt Pantel groups the banquets with various social practices that define the *koinon*, the common or public domain, in contrast to the *idion*, the particular or private sphere. *Koinon* practices include the bearing of arms and participation in collective hunting, religious rituals, and banquets (110); all of these activities concur in defining and enhancing citizenship in the polis. Archaic Greece sees no sharp distinction between political institutions proper, such as the assemblies at the Agora, and other elements of public life, such as the banquets (112).

The banquets have their origin in the religious sacrifice (*thusía*) of a bull or ox that is ritually killed, then cooked, and eventually divided among the participants. According to a detailed description of the ritual, "the group of citizens is not constituted upon the death of the animal ... this happens rather with the commensality around the pieces of beef.... All those who eat become citizens.... Eating is definitely the main event.... The city emerges because it eats beef."[5] In this manner, commensality is explicitly related to the birth of political community.

A slight change in the function of banquets occurs in Athens during the classical period (fifth century). A certain type of commensality is now reserved for specific occasions: the fifty citizens (*prytans*) who represent the city of Athens after the democratic reforms of Kleisthenes are strictly obliged to eat together at the Tholos, a central circular building near the Agora. But the classical period did not produce a real break in the forms and functions of the banquet in general; it retains and even reinforces its role as the principal place where sociability is being "fermented" (Fustel de Coulanges) and where various rituals are being performed. The common meal becomes institutionalized as a symbol of the permanence of political power in a democracy (170). Later on, during the Hellenistic period, the banquets are increasingly organized and financed by benefactors belonging to the most powerful and wealthy families (*évergétes*) in various Greek

22

cities (410), as is attested by numerous inscriptions (Veyne 1976; also Gautier 1985, 147–66; Sartre 1991, 147–66; Andreau, Schmitt, and Schnapp 1978).

Throughout, Schmitt Pantel emphasizes the close connection between the commensality of the banquet and the resulting social and citizen relationships: "There is a direct tie between the practices of commensality and the functioning of power and the type of politics" (438). The banquet occupies a key position connecting what we would call today the religious, the public, and the private spheres (250). For the classical period Schmitt Pantel quotes writers from Euripides to Plato and Aristotle, showing that "commensality is the tie of friendship which is formed and becomes stronger during the practice of common banquets. Commensality in turn allows *philia* (friendship) which guarantees not so much the social order, but the consensus that is necessary to life in society.... Both Aristotle and Plato... show the considerable extent to which the forms of commensality were in classical Athens an integral part of a reflection on the *politeia*" (488). The banquet was the preeminent expression of what we like to call today "civil society."

Schmitt Pantel asserts that the intriguing title of her own work, *La Cité au banquet* (The city at the banquet), is at least as justified in characterizing life in ancient Athens as the frequently used expression "The City at the Agora." For her title reflects perhaps more exactly the evolution of social relations in the city (490). Her final plea (*ibid.*) is "to take commensality seriously" (*prendre la commensalité au sérieux*) — as she places this passage in quotes, she may here be paraphrasing the title of Ronald Dworkin's *Taking Rights Seriously* (1978).

In this spirit, I am tempted to suggest that a direct link exists between the banquet and the emergence of Athenian democracy, that towering political invention of the Greeks. Schmitt Pantel does not quite venture this thought, but other prominent members of the modern French classical school have done so squarely. In a long preface to a dissertation dealing in detail with the ritual sacrifice and slaughter of oxen during the banquets in ancient Greece, Marcel Detienne (1982) writes: "After the sacrifice, the animal is carved up through egalitarian division: the isonomic model is applied and commensality takes place through a procedure which makes for portions of equal size and weight being distributed by means of sortition" (Berthiaume 1982). And Nicole Loraux (1981), another prominent Hellenist, contends in a well-known review article: "To eat equal portions means to produce and to reproduce political equality; in the communal meal arises the isonomic figure of the city." Yet another French scholar, referring to Plutarch's *Table Talks*, writes similarly that "we know that the essentially democratic procedure of sortition (i.e., lottery) was utilized to assure that the portions of beef were distributed equitably" (Durand 1997, 154).[6]

"Isonomy" is the classical Greek term for equality before the law. It also refers to equal distribution of various political offices by lottery or sortition rather than through elections. Sortition was the crucial mechanism for the selection (and regular rotation) of the principal polis officials and magistrates (except for military leaders) in the Athenian democracy, as Bernard Manin (1995, 19–61) emphasizes. Apparently, equal division of the ritually sacrificed oxen among banquet members led in Athens, through a remarkable association of ideas, to the equal distribution of offices among the citizens through lottery.

One might object at this point that there is a substantial difference between the equitable carving up of an ox among the members of a banquet and the distribution of a limited number of polis offices among the citizens by means of a lottery: there were always many more citizens than offices, while the number of

24

meat portions was necessarily equal to that of the participants in a banquet. Yet the task of dividing an ox into approximately equal pieces among the participants required a highly skilled operation on the part of the butcher; in a way, this division was more complex than the outright elimination from public office through lottery of a given number of polis members, especially if the selection for such offices was made for relatively short periods (say, one year) and if the principle of periodic rotation was strictly applied, as came to be the case in Athens. In this manner, "isonomy" came to be the rule of the polity as much as of the banquet.

I agree with Manin (1995, 41–42) that the designation of polis officials through lottery did not have a religious, sacerdotal origin or function, as had been held by Fustel de Coulanges and Gustave Glotz. But the use and importance of lottery in Athenian democracy owes much to its similarity with the banquet procedure. It would seem that Simmel was right: if Athenian democracy was one of its externalities or side-effects, the sociological-political significance of the meal or banquet was truly immense.

Symposium, *Männerbund*, and Beer Drinking in German Student Corporations

In a book on development projects (Hirschman 1968, ch. 5), I have made much of the "centrality of side-effects." The story I have just told about Greek banquets illustrates this concept: a bloody religious sacrifice had a remarkable and remarkably positive outcome in the field of politics. But this relationship cannot be expected to have been the rule. A rather different story seems to be in the offing in a paper by the well-known Oxford University Hellenist Oswyn Murray (1982). Under the title "Symposium and Männerbund," he would surely describe, one might think, the sharp contrast between the Greek banquet and the Germanic *Männerbund*. In fact, Murray does nothing of the kind.

25

Rather, he adverts to the undoubted structural similarity between the two institutions: both are associations of young men outside of kinship groups, both practice homosexuality and engage in communal eating and drinking, and both have religious origins and perform religious and warlike functions. Strangely, Murray does not mention the spectacular contrast between the socio-political connotations and characteristics of symposium and *Männerbund*: the dawn of democracy in classical Greece, on the one hand, and the raging (*wütig*) fury of wild, plundering bands of young men (*Berserker*) in ancient Germany and Scandinavia, on the other (see Dumézil 1939, 91; Weiser 1927; Höfler 1934). One cannot help thinking of the *Männerbund* as foreboding some of the worst aspects of Germany's later political developments, such as the murderous activities of the post-1918 "Free Corps" and the subsequent SA and SS movements of the Nazi period.[7]

Such perhaps fanciful, yet irresistible historical connections aside, the social psychology of communal drinking (rather than eating) is penetratingly explored in Heinrich Mann's best-known novel, *Der Untertan* (The Subject).[8] This story takes place in Imperial Germany just before World War I. Its key turning point occurs early in the novel when the principal character, the weak, mendacious, craven, and all-round contemptible Diederich Hessling joins a group of students, the "Neoteutonic Corporation," and engages with them in frequent, ritualized beer drinking. This activity does not stop him from being utterly contemptible, but he now manages to hide his self-doubts and numerous other vices and weaknesses, becomes remarkably assertive, and eventually achieves worldly "success." Here is how Heinrich Mann describes the transformation of his antihero:

[He] had become a 'Konkneipant' [member of a group going regularly to a *Kneipe*, or bar] — he felt predestined for this task. He now

26

belonged to a large group of people where nobody...demanded anything from him except drinking. Full of gratitude and benevolence he raised his glass to anyone who did the same. To drink, not to drink, to sit, to stand, to talk or to sing did no longer depend on him. All of these activities were loudly ordered and properly carried out and thus one lived in peace with oneself and the world.... Diederich was immersed in the corporation which did his thinking and desiring for him. As a member of the corporation he now became a man with self-respect — and because he belonged to it he also turned into a man of honor....

Beer! Alcohol! There one sat and could always have more. Beer was not like those coquettish, demanding women, it was faithful (*treu*) and cozy (*gemütlich*).With beer there was no need to act, to achieve, as with women. Everything happened of its own accord: one swallowed and with that one already had achieved something, one felt transported to the heights of existence, felt like a free man, free from the inner point of view (*innerlich frei*) — the beer one swallowed was transformed into internal freedom. And one virtually had already passed one's exams. One was 'through,' was a doctor! (Mann 1918, 29–32.)

Once again, sociologically it was highly significant to gather together a social group that ate or, in this case, drank in common. Obviously, those who did so did not truly acquire self-respect, honor, and "inner freedom" in the process. Rather, by drinking beer with their fellow students, the likes of Diederich could *pretend* to have these desirable qualities, they could feign and fake them.

Here then is a case where commensality generates externalities of a socially negative kind. Just as Simmel underlines the social *benefits* of joining in a common meal, Heinrich Mann describes the opposite phenomenon, the lamentable result of becoming a "Konkneipant." In their own ways, however, and at about the same time, both Simmel and Heinrich Mann converged on the impact, positive or negative, of the joint consumption of food or drink.

Actually, the difference between Simmel and Mann is not as wide as one might think. True, at the beginning of his essay, Simmel emphasizes the tendency of the meal to rise from its "physiological primitiveness" to the complex and noble sphere of "social interactions." But, as already noted, he later places ceilings on this upward movement as he stresses and vindicates the "banality of table conversation" with its "generality and lack of intimacy." Here Simmel suddenly accepts and even advocates a narrow boundary to the fine human and social relations that are apt to arise during the *Mahlzeit* — a boundary drawn against the hypocrisy and vulgarity characteristic of human relations in the Wilhelmine Kneipe of Heinrich Mann.

Economists (including both Scitovsky and myself) have often looked at the consumption of food as a purely private and self-centered activity, with the ensuing relief of hunger and enjoyment of nourishment being a positive but decreasing function of spending on food. In the middle of the nineteenth century, the German statistician Ernst Engel (1821–96) demonstrated this functional relationship, and it seemed so reliable that it soon became known and celebrated as "Engel's Law." But to confine the consequences of food intake solely to the concurrent biological process of satiation means overlooking the considerable public dimension of commensality.

While they are consuming food and drink, people gathering for the *Mahlzeit* engage in conversation and discussion, exchange information and points of view, tell stories, perform religious services, and so on. From the purely biological point of view, there is no doubt that eating has a straightforward relationship to individual welfare. But once they are done *in common*, eating and drinking normally go hand in hand with a remarkably diverse set of public or collective activities. That is why "taking commensality seriously"—as Pauline Schmitt Pantel has urged—is easier said than done. The social, political, and cultural consequences of the common meal are extraordinarily varied; moreover, their outcome can turn out to be positive or negative. The common meal or banquet contributed to the "invention" of democracy in the age of classical Athens, on the one hand; in the Imperial Germany of Heinrich Mann, on the other, commensality could lead to the degradation of human relations and political life.

NOTES

The author thanks Pauline Schmitt Pantel, Marcel Detienne, and Bernard Manin for numerous discussions.

1. See also Bell 1985 and Feeley-Harnik 1981.

2. Rabelais, *Pantagruel*, I. See also Jeanneret 1991, 27.

3. I briefly noted the similarity between Pascal's argument and the economist's definition of public goods in Hirschman 1971.

4. My emphasis. The original German version of this essay has been reprinted as Simmel 1984. An English translation was recently published as an annex to Symons 1994 (333–51). I came across this article in German and was much taken by it several years ago. Thinking it had still not been translated, I decided to undertake this job in the spring of 1995 in Berlin. I am using my unpublished translation here.

5. Schmitt Pantel 444, quoting Durand 1926, 64–65.

6. See also *Plutarch's Table Talks*, II, 10,642 e–f.

7. On the ferocity of the "Free Corps," the SA, and the SS, see Waite 1952 and Theweleit 1977. The connection between the archaic Germanic *Männerbund* and the extreme right-wing movements in Germany during the 1920s and 1930s has been made explicitly in Dumézil 1939. In 1985 Carlo Ginzburg criticized this book for its pro-Nazi sympathies. Dumézil replied briefly (1985). After Dumézil's death in 1986, the journalist Didier Eribon (1992) wrote at

length in Dumézil's defense. A brief rejoinder by Ginzburg appeared in *Le Monde des Débats* in September 1993, and a further rejoinder by Eribon in the same magazine in October 1993.

8. Mann 1918 was completed shortly before the outbreak of World War I. See also Gillot 1992.

REFERENCES

Andreau, Jean, Pauline Schmitt, and Alain Schnapp. 1978. "Paul Veyne et l'Evergétisme." *Annales ESC*, no. 33 (janvier–février).

Baumol, William. 1995. "The Case for Subsidizing the Arts" (interview). *Challenge* (Sept.–Oct.): 52–56.

Bell, Rudoph M. 1985. *Holy Anorexia*. Chicago: University of Chicago Press.

Berthiaume, Guy. 1982. *Les Rôles du Mágeiros*. Leiden: E.J. Brill. Preface by Marcel Detienne.

Bynum, Caroline Walker. 1987. *Holy Feast and Holy Fast: The Religious Significance of Food to Medieval Women*. Berkeley: University of California Press.

Detienne, Marcel, J.P. Vernant, et al. 1979. *La Cuisine du sacrifice en pays grec*. Paris: Gallimard.

Dorfman, Robert. 1969. "General Equilibrium with Public Goods." In J. Margolis and H. Guitton, eds., *Public Economics*. New York: St. Martin Press.

Dumézil, Georges. 1939. *Mythes et Dieux des Germains*. Paris: Libraire Ernest Leroux.

Dumézil, Georges. 1985. "Science et politique: Réponse à Carlo Ginzburg." *Annales ESC*, no. 5 (Sept.–Oct.): 985–89.

Durand, Jean-Louis. 1926. *Sacrifice et labour en Grèce ancienne*. Paris and Rome: Editions de la Découverte.

Durand, Jean-Louis. 1979. "Bêtes Grecques." In Detienne, Vernant, et al. 1979.

Eribon, Didier. 1992. *Faut-il brûler Dumézil?* Paris: Flammarion.

Feeley-Harnik, Gillian. 1981. *The Lord's Table: Eucharist and Passover in Early Christianity*. Philadelphia: University of Pennsylvania Press.

Gautier, Philippe. 1985. *Les Cités grecques et leurs bienfaiteurs*. Athens: Ecole Française d' Athénes.

Ginzburg, Carlo. 1985. "Mythologie Germanique et Nazisme: Sur un ancien livre de Georges Dumézil." *Annales ESC*, no. 4 (July–Aug.)

Hirschman, Albert O. 1995. *A Propensity to Self-Subversion*. Cambridge, MA: Harvard University Press.

Hirschman, Albert O. 1971. *A Bias for Hope: Essays on Development and Latin America* . New Haven: Yale University Press.

Hirschman, Albert O. 1968. *Development Projects Observed*. Washington, D.C.: Brookings Institution.

Hirschman, Albert O. 1982. *Shifting Involvements: Private Interest and Public Action*. Princeton: Princeton University Press.

Höfler, Otto. 1934. *Kultische Geheimbünde der Germanen*, vol. I. Frankfurt: Diesterweg.

Jeanneret, Michel. 1991. *A Feast of Words: Banquets and Table Talk in the Renaissance*. Chicago: University of Chicago Press

Loraux, Nicole. 1981. "La Cité comme cuisine et comme partage." *Annales ESC*.

Manin, Bernard. 1995. *Principes du gouvernement représentatif*. Paris: Calmann Levy.

Mann, Heinrich. 1918. *Der Untertan*. Leipzig: Wolff.

Montaigne, Michel. 1933. *Essais*. Paris: Bibliothèque de la Pléiade.

Morineau, Michel. 1987. "La Douceur d'être inclus." In Françoise Thélamon, ed., *Sociabilité, pouvoirs et société*. Université de Rouen, Publication No. 110,

Murray, Oswyn. 1982. "Symposium and Männerbund." Concilium Eirene, XVI, ed. P. Oliva.

Pascal, Blaise. 1969. *Oeuvres Complètes*. Paris: Bibliothèque de la Pléiade.

Rabelais. 1934. *Oeuvres Complètes*. Paris: Bibliothèque de la Pléiade.

Rostow, W.W. 1960. *Stages of Economic Growth*. Cambridge: Cambridge University Press.

Sartre, Maurice. 1991. *L'Orient romain*. Paris: Seuil.

Samuelson, Paul A. 1954. "The Pure Theory of Public Expenditure." *Review of Economics and Statistics* 36: 387–89.

Samuelson, Paul A. 1955. "Diagrammatic Exposition of a Theory of Public Expenditure." *Review of Economics and Statistics* 37: 350–56.

Schmitt Pantel, Pauline. 1992. *La Cité au banquet: Histoire des repas publics dans les cités grecques.* Rome: Ecole Française de Rome.

Scitovsky, Tibor. 1976. *The Joyless Economy.* New York: Oxford University Press.

Simmel, Georg. 1984. *Das Individuum und die Freiheit: Essais.* Berlin: Wagenbach

Symons, Michael. 1994. "Simmel's Gastronomic Sociology: An Overlooked Essay." *Food and Foodways* 5, no. 4:333–51.

Theweleit, Klaus. 1987. *Male Phantasies,* 2 vols. Minneapolis: University of Minnesota Press.

Throsby, David. 1994. "The Production and Consumption of the Arts: A View of Cultural Economics." *Journal of Economic Literature* 32 (Mar.): 1-29.

Veyne, Paul. 1976. *Le Pain et le cirque.* Paris: Seuil.

Waite, Robert G.L. 1952. *Vanguard of Nazism: The Free Corps Movement of Postwar Germany.* New York: W.W. Norton.

Weiser, Lily. *Altgermanische Jünglingsweihen und Männerbünde.* Baden.

CHAPTER TWO

Fifty Years After the Marshall Plan:

Two Posthumous Memoirs and

Some Personal Recollections

I well remember the occasion, exactly ten years ago, when there were numerous celebrations of the *fortieth* anniversary of the Marshall Plan. When I inquired about the reason for this vogue, the explanation was simple and convincing: Forty years after the event, so I was told, many of the people who took an important part in it, are still "around," and may have interesting stories to tell, having been at their best — that is, from thirty to forty years old — at the time of the event that is to be commemorated. But for this very reason, most of these people are likely to be "gone" by the time the fiftieth anniversary rolls around. Now, *fifty* years later, I cannot but recognize that we do suffer from this age-related comparative disadvantage in relation to the groups that met ten years ago. It occurred to me, however, that, in compensation, our group may count on a quite temporary, but real comparative advantage: by the time we are scheduled to talk, some important participants in the events may well have departed, but at the same time they may have left behind some recollections or memoirs that were not available ten years earlier. Indeed, today we can take advantage of precisely this situation: two of the key actors of the Marshall Plan, Robert Marjolin on the European-French side and Richard Bissell on the United States side, did die within the past decade, but both left behind almost finished memoirs, which were easy to put together in book form. Let me rapidly recall who these people were.

Robert Marjolin, who had worked as an economist and journal editor before the war, joined the "Free French" movement of General de Gaulle after the French debacle of 1940 and spent much of the war in London and Washington, where he became a close collaborator of Jean Monnet, who was then head of the French purchasing mission in the United States. When, just after the end of the war in Europe, de Gaulle was president of France, Jean Monnet was placed in charge of a new plan for "Equipment and Modernization" and Marjolin followed as Monnet's deputy. With France already having its own program for national recovery, it was natural for this mechanism to be utilized when Western Europe as a whole was called upon by the Marshall Plan to establish a joint recovery plan. Thus Marjolin was appointed secretary general and was in fact the guiding spirit of the Organization for European Economic Cooperation (OEEC) from 1946 to 1955 and later became vice president of the European Economic Community, from 1958 to 1967. His book was published posthumously under the fitting title *Le Travail d'une vie* (Paris: Robert Laffont, 1986).

Richard Bissell had been a professor of economics at MIT before the war, then joined the War Shipping Administration during the war and the Office of Mobilization and Reconversion during the transition to a peace economy. Paul Hoffman, an important automobile manufacturer, was appointed in 1948 as the first Marshall Plan Administrator, or the director of the newly established Economic Cooperation Administration (ECA). He asked Bissell to join him as the deputy and assistant administrator for programs. Bissell became the recognized intellectual leader and a forceful spokesman for the agency during congressional hearings for the organization. His posthumous memoirs were strikingly entitled *Reflections of a Cold Warrior* (New Haven and London: Yale University Press, 1996). But this title was selected, so I understand, by Yale University Press rather than by Bissell himself, and it reflects primarily the post–Marshall Plan part of his career. In 1954 he joined the CIA, where he organized the U-2 overflights and later was responsible for the disastrous Bay of Pigs operation in Cuba. These events did eclipse, for the general public in the United States, the remarkable role Bissell had played earlier in Europe. But those who knew him at the time tend rather to agree with what he wrote himself in introducing his own brilliant chapter on the Marshall Plan: "The challenge and stimulation I knew I would experience convinced me to postpone academia.... [W]hat followed were perhaps the most worthwhile years of my career" (Bissell, p. 29).

It would be tempting to write a paper for this occasion, with the exclusive purpose of comparing the chapters of the Marjolin and Bissell books that deal with the Marshall Plan. I shall do so at the beginning but various personal recollections will occasionally intrude into the account. Superficially, our two principal actors had a great deal in common. Both men had arrived at similarly key positions at approximately the same youngish age (Marjolin at thirty-nine years, Bissell at forty-one). Both were economists, with, as was normal during the period immediately after World War II, a strong background in Keynesian doctrine and a consequent belief in the value of governmental activism. But the early pages of these books immediately bring out substantial differences in educational and social backgrounds. Bissell belonged typically to the upper middle class. His father was an important insurance executive living in Hartford, Connecticut. According to traditional patterns, Bissell went to Groton for high school and to Yale for college. Then, at the height of the Depression, he spent a year at the London School of Economics. About this period he writes: "I went to London as a Republican simply as a matter of inherited political allegiance. Roosevelt's campaign and then his first months in office had an impact. I felt very strongly that many of the things he did were constructive and necessary and I came to believe in the importance of that type of government intervention in the economy" (Bissell, p. 11). The next year he returned to the United States to continue studying economics at Yale and soon came to teach, with considerable success, Yale's first course in Keynesian economics.

In contrast to Bissell, Marjolin received anything but an orthodox education. The great surprise of his book for his older friends such as myself was the extremely low social and economic level from which he had risen and which today would classify him firmly among the category now known in France as "les exclus" (the "excluded ones") and in this country as the "underclass." But fortunately, these terms had not yet been invented, and Marjolin describes fascinatingly, in the first fifty pages of his book, how he managed to "catch up" — largely outside the formal school system. The story is rather like the one told so movingly by Albert Camus in his recent posthumous novel *Le Premier homme* (published in English as *The First Man*). Both Marjolin and Camus describe how their mothers made ends meet by taking in laundry. In both careers, decisive roles are played by teachers or mentors who recognized the talents of the young men.

Here, I shall insert a brief autobiographical paragraph: I met Marjolin first in Paris, in 1938, when Mussolini's new anti-Semitic decrees compelled me to return to France after two years in Italy. This was my second emigration: my first had taken place in 1933, when, following Hitler's ascent to power, I had left my native Berlin for Paris. By the time I returned to Paris I was twenty-three years old, and Marjolin gave me my first job as the Italian specialist of *L'Activité Economique*, a quarterly review on recent economic trends in Europe, which he published for the new Rockefeller Foundation–financed Institut de Recherches Economiques et Sociales. At twenty-eight years, he did not show any traces of his unorthodox upbringing; rather, he seemed to me by then a true *patron* (or boss), perhaps a bit too cordial to a newcomer like myself. Only when I was allowed to meet the actual *patron de la maison*, who was none other than Charles Rist, the eminent economist and former governor of the Bank of France, did I realize that there were many shades of *patrons* in this world.

With their duties and responsibilities being so parallel during the Marshall Plan, I was curious to find out, first of all, what these two men, Bissell and Marjolin, had to say about each other in their books. The outcome of this inquiry was actually disappointing. Bissell's activity was primarily in the Washington theater. This may in part account for the fact that Marjolin's name does not even appear in the index. On the other hand, Marjolin has some quite warm words for Bissell: "In Washington . . . we also met again with Richard Bissell. . . . His considerable intellectual abilities and the warmth of his feelings toward Europe contributed a great deal to the success of the enterprise." Marjolin has similarly kind and well-chosen words for Paul Hoffman, Lincoln Gordon, Edmund Hall-Patch, and particularly for Eric Roll. He ends up this passage about his collaborators by declaring: "Never in my experience, before and after the Marshall Plan, have I known an international team animated by such an intense desire to achieve success in a common enterprise" (Marjolin, p. 196).

There was another topic on which I was curious to compare Bissell's and Marjolin's accounts: the European Payments Union, in whose negotiation I became deeply involved. I shall introduce it by way of another bit of autobiography. After having been discharged from the American Army in 1945, I started working, in the following year, at the Federal Reserve Board in Washington, where it was my initial task to follow economic and financial events in France and Italy. I soon became responsible for Western Europe as a whole, and to the extent the Federal Reserve had a role in U.S. foreign economic policy, the Marshall Plan became my area of competence. In particular, I became interested in the plans for Intra-European Payments and in the various attempts to move away from the strict bilateral channels to which trade and payments in Europe were then still confined.

This was the second important area where Marshall's principle that Europe was expected to come up with an agreement on the subdivision of American dollars was invoked. First of all, the Western European countries were to get together and to present jointly an estimate of the help that was needed from the United States. This task was accomplished fairly rapidly: the Committee of European Economic Cooperation (CEEC) was formed in Paris and it completed its report by September 1947. With the Congress passing the needed authorizations and appropriations, large-scale aid was flowing to Europe by the middle of 1948.

The next task was the reconstruction of multilateral trade in Europe. Here, in principle, the idea was again that the Europeans should come forward with a joint proposal for what was called, rather ambiguously, the further "integration" of Europe. But, by this time, the Marshall Plan agency in Washington and its new Paris branch had come into flourishing bureaucratic existence and they, together with what had now been renamed the Office of European Economic Cooperation (OEEC) in Paris, participated fully in the "idea mongering" that went on in various attempts to come forward with the best conceivable formulas.

To acquire some proficiency in this area, I soon discovered that to do my job adequately, I had better get to know the actual policy makers in this area in Washington. They were a small group of people around Bissell, a so-called brain trust, which fed various new institutional ideas to him, and through him to the Paris office of the new Marshall Plan agency, the Economic Cooperation Administration (ECA). I became quite friendly with this group, whose original members were Van (Harold Van Buren) Cleveland and Ted (Theodore) Geiger. Later on, this group was joined by another young man, John Hulley. I came to spend a good deal of time with these people, so that my office was virtually transplanted from the Federal Reserve Board to the new ECA building. I much enjoyed taking part in this manner in the "activism" of this group, which constantly invented new functions for the Marshall Plan and its dollars.

As an example, and because of its timeliness now, when the "Euro" is about to be launched, I will recall that, back in December 1949, I prepared a paper entitled "Proposal for a European Monetary Authority," where I presented a fairly detailed survey of the common fiscal, monetary, and foreign exchange policies that might be adopted gradually under the guidance of a future European Central Bank. The paper was circulated within the ECA. A note written by Van Cleveland introduced me as a staff member of the Federal Reserve Board and explained that the paper was circulated "in response to an informal request." Cleveland was a member of our brain trust and was identified in his note as "program secretary" in the ECA. The note also took care to add that the views expressed were "not necessarily those of the Federal Reserve Board." [This paper has not been published, except for an Italian translation, "Proposta per una Autorità Monetaria Europea." See Luca Meldolesi, ed., *Albert O. Hirschman: Tre Continenti* (Torino: Giulio Einaudi, 1990), pp. 7–18.]

The most important function of our group was to work on a plan for setting up and improving a new intra-European payments scheme — the European Payments Union, soon to be known as EPU. At an early stage I did not realize that this activity would eventually produce a conflict between my new role as informal adviser to the ECA and my bureaucratic position as a staff member of the Federal Reserve Board. The international division of the board to which I belonged was headed first by Frank Southard, who later became the U.S. representative on the executive board of the International Monetary Fund (IMF), and then by Arthur Marget. Both men were highly critical of the new functions that the ECA was proposing for the European Payments Union and which they saw as conflicting with the principles and expected role of the International Monetary Fund. By the time the positions of the various U.S. agencies participating in international economic policy making (the members of the National Advisory Council for International Monetary and Financial Affairs) had become clear, my point of view coincided with that of the ECA. That view wholly supported the European Payments Union, but was opposed vehemently by the Treasury and, to a somewhat smaller degree, by the Federal Reserve. In the end, the Economic Cooperation Administration view prevailed, largely because Paul Hoffman's role was paramount. In October 1949, he had gone to Paris to deliver a rousing speech in which he appealed to the need for European "integration" no less than fifteen times, as Bissell points out emphatically (Bissell, p. 63). With the European Payments Union standing as the current symbol for "integration," it won out over the doubters and skeptics.

If we now look at the views on the European Payments Union as expressed by Bissell and Marjolin a considerable time after the events, we are struck by how strongly favorable their opinion has remained. Bissell wrote: "Under the direction of a managing board, the EPU created a clearing mechanism for payments made in any European currency. With all European currencies readily transferable, the barriers of bilateral trade arrangements were broken.... I have always felt that the EPU *was in some ways the supreme organizational achievement of the Marshall Plan"* (Bissell, p. 64, emphasis added). Yet, just a page later, Bissell concedes that this action was taken by the Economic Co-operation Administration "in total disregard of standing U.S. policy, which strongly supported multilateralism, and in spite of opposition from the Treasury, which understandably was *infuriated"* (my emphasis). This episode, as Bissell so well describes it, taught me much about how decisions are actually made in Washington, in spite of elaborate arrangements for "interagency coordination" and lip service to it.

As for Marjolin, his admiration for the American (i.e., ECA) initiative in pushing the European Payments Union through is even more striking. He writes:

> On no other question did the postwar American policy manifest itself with greater brilliance. Not only did the United States grant at the time massive financial aid to their allies and former enemies making thus possible...the economic recovery of the most developed region outside of the United States which would one day foreseeably become a formidable competitor, but it pushed and jostled the Europeans to unite and to increase in this way their economic and political strength. To be more precise, the United States pushed the European countries to create a system of payments which restored the convertibility of their currencies into each other while excluding the convertibility of these currencies into the dollar. Even more, the United States virtually forced the Europeans to free a considerable portion of their imports from other European countries while accepting that import restrictions on the same products be maintained when they originated in the United States. This way of acting unselfishly, *while apparently absurd*, would bear its fruits. In

the course of the fifties, Europe's payments to the rest of the world could increasingly be paid without recourse to American aid until general convertibility, including the dollar, could be restored in 1958. Progressively, the discriminatory measures against American foreign trade would be abolished.... The sort of *wager* the Americans had made in the last ten years had therefore been won. In the course of history, it is rare to see long-term and highly uncertain benefits accrue so neatly. (Marjolin, pp. 217–18, emphasis added.)

Marjolin's comment was most thoughtful in characterizing the European Payments Union as an "apparently absurd, but successful wager" that permitted and encouraged temporary discrimination against the dollar. Viewed from this angle, it was a different and higher form of altruism than simple commodity aid, which had been the essence of Marshall aid. It permitted and encouraged temporary discrimination against imports from the United States. This exception to the rule of nondiscrimination explains also why the arrangement aroused such unremitting hostility on the part of some sections of our own government, not to speak of the recently created International Monetary Fund. In closing this chapter, Marjolin points to the direct connection between the Marshall Plan and the European Payments Union, on the one hand, and the Treaty of Rome and the European Customs Union ten years later (pp. 220–21).

Today these positive appraisals of the European Payments Union by Bissell and Marjolin make me feel good. But at the time, my personal position was becoming ever more difficult. As Bissell remarked, the United States had pushed through a policy that "infuriated" not only the Treasury, but also its allies within the government, such as the Federal Reserve, where I was still working. The positions I had taken made me feel increasingly uncomfortable. When, after a while, the opportunity arose to leave Washington, I seized it with much relief. Recommended by the World Bank, I decided to move to Bogotá, Colombia, as an economic and financial adviser to the government there. Little did I appreciate then how this move would start an entirely new phase of my life. Yet, some of the key notions of my later writings on development, such as a "Passion for the Possible" and a "Bias for Hope," may go back to Marjolin's concept of "an apparently absurd, but successful wager," which for him was a principal characteristic of the Marshall Plan.

BIBLIOGRAPHICAL NOTE

The principal sources for this paper are the above-noted books by Richard Bissell and Robert Marjolin, plus my memory. In addition, the following items have been found useful:

Diebold, William, Jr. *Trade and Payments in Western Europe: A Study in Economic Cooperation, 1947–51.* New York: Harper & Brothers, 1952.

Eichengreen, Barry, ed. *The Reconstruction of the International Economy, 1945–1960.* Brookfield, VT: Elgar Reference Collection, 1996.

Hinshaw, Randall. *Toward European Convertibility: Essays in International Finance,* no. 31, Nov. 1958. Princeton: Princeton University Press.

Hirschman, Albert O. "The European Payments Union: Negotiations and Issues." *Review of Economics and Statistics* 33, no. 1 (Feb. 1951): 49–55; also reprinted in Eichengreen, ed., pp. 323–29.

Hoffmann, Stanley and Charles Maier, eds. *The Marshall Plan: A Retrospective.* Boulder, CO, and London: Westview Press, 1984.

Kaplan, Jacob J., and Günther Schleminger. *The European Payments Union: Financial Diplomacy in the 1950s.* Oxford: Clarendon Press, 1989.

Kindleberger, Charles P. *Marshall Plan Days.* Boston: Allen & Unwin, 1987.

Meldolesi, Luca. *Albert O. Hirschman: Tre Continenti.* Torino: Giulio Enaudi, 1990.

Wexler, Imanuel. *The Marshall Plan Revisited: The European Recovery Program in Economic Perspective.* Westport, CT: Greenwood Press, 1983.

CHAPTER THREE

Trespassing: Places and Ideas

in the Course of a Life

Part One
The European Years

Let's start from the beginning: Tell us something about your origins.
I was born in Berlin to a middle-class family of Jewish origin, but
did not practice the Jewish religion. Actually, both my sisters and
I were baptized as Protestants. At that time — I was born in 1915,
during the First World War — it was a rather common thing among
emancipated German Jews to be baptized in the Protestant church;
but I think it is important to add that this did not mean there was
any religious tension in our upbringing. During a certain period
of my life I felt close to a primitive form of Christianity; that was
when I was reading a great deal of Tolstoy. But I never went regularly to any Protestant church, and I was never confirmed. I did
my secondary studies at the Französische Gymnasium in Berlin —
an excellent school — and spent nine years of my life there, until
graduation. Some three hundred years ago this school had been
founded in Prussia for the Huguenots who had taken refuge there,
fleeing religious persecution in France; later the school was run
by the Prussian state. I received a good education there, mainly
in French, but also in classical languages, such as Latin and Greek.
However, English was not taught.

What did your father do?

He was a surgeon and specialized in neurosurgery. He was very devoted to his work. His family came from Eastern Germany, and in fact my father had been born in the region of Poznan, the part of Germany that was ceded to Poland after World War I. He died of cancer in March 1933, just after Hitler took power. I must say that it was the coincidence of his death with the anti-democratic and anti-Semitic persecutions that made me decide to leave Germany and to go to France. My mother, however, remained in Germany. I chose France mainly because I spoke French rather well. France had been part of my education, one might say.

And your mother?

My mother came from a big family, a large tribe; she had many brothers and cousins. Before marrying my father, she had been married once before; strangely, her first husband's name was also Hirschmann. My mother had studied history of art and history, the kinds of things a woman could study at the time, and had lived on her own in Strasbourg and Munich. In short, she was from an emancipated milieu. Then she returned to Berlin, where she married my father. His colleagues and friends were not only Jews; I remember that one of his closest friends was from El Salvador.

What was the atmosphere at home? What kinds of people visited your house?

My parents' friends were mostly doctors and lawyers, but there were also some art dealers — among them I recall the Tannhausers, who were owners of a famous gallery (they later left their collection to the Guggenheim Museum). We lived in a nice apartment in a quarter of Berlin known as the Alte Westen, which adjoined the Tiergarten, Berlin's famous central park. We did not have a garden, but the Greek Embassy was next to our house, and it had a courtyard where we were often allowed to play ball. Our apartment was very simple and lacked certain elements of modern comfort: we heated with coal, there was no running water except for a bathtub, and we washed in washbasins filled with pitchers of water. When I arrived in Paris, everything seemed suddenly much more modern. Anyway, we led the life of a middle-class family. In the summer we always went on vacation, first to Heringsdorf, a beach resort on the Baltic, when we were quite young, then to the North Sea, and still later to places in Switzerland and Austria, or even to the Dolomites, in Italy.

And your two sisters?
The eldest, Ursula, was only about one year older than me, and she was the person with whom I shared some of the most important events in my life, from 1915 to 1935, when she married her first husband, Eugenio Colorni, a philosopher and antifascist. From 1935 to 1938 Ursula lived in Italy, first with Colorni in Trieste, and then mostly in forced exile on the island of Ventotene until 1944, when Colorni was killed in Rome by the fascists. Her second husband was Altiero Spinelli, the European federalist. Spinelli died in 1986 and Ursula in 1991. She left a fine book of memoirs, published posthumously under the title *Noi senza patria* [We without a fatherland] [Bologna: Il Mulino, 1993], in which she recounts many episodes of our family life and our adolescence.

Then I have another sister, Eva, who lives in Rome and is five years younger than me. When I left Germany I was eighteen years old and she was thirteen, but she is still my "little sister" even though she is now seventy-seven years old!

Which languages did you speak in the family? When did you learn English?
English was the fourth or fifth language I learned. The first was, of course, German, the second French, the third Italian, and then came English and Spanish.

And Yiddish?
No, I never learned it, I only know a few words.

But you spoke French at home?
No, we just spoke it with a French demoiselle whom we had hired in Paris and who lived with us for a year or so, to teach us the language.

Were politics discussed at home?
Yes, but it was hardly the principal topic. However, all of us started to speak about politics after 1930, because that year — I was fifteen years old — the Nazis won their first big election victory.

By the way, in the Französische Gymnasium I had some friends who were older than me and one in particular had a certain influence on me; he made me read Marx when I was fourteen years old. He was my mentor, and his name was Heinrich Ehrmann. In Germany, the figure of the mentor was important. In 1931 I joined the youth movement of the Social Democratic Party, as far as I remember as a result of conversations with Heinrich Ehrmann. From then on we have followed more or less the same itinerary: he also went first to France and in 1940 left for the United States, where he became a political scientist.

Tell us some more about how you joined the socialist youth movement. Was your sister Ursula the first to enter?
No, I joined first and she followed later.

Did you have any important teachers during this period of your life?
As I said before, I had a few important teachers. One was a teacher
of religion who made me read Tolstoy's short stories; he was an
excellent person who later opposed the Nazis. Then I had an excellent teacher of German; he was Jewish, but remained in Germany. The German he spoke was extraordinary. I do not know
how he managed to survive. He was totally devoted to teaching
literature: "As to Goethe's *Faust*," he used to say, "it's impossible
to read it in school. If you want to learn it, come to my house and
we'll read it together." We then formed a collective work group,
an *Arbeitsgemeinschaft*. For an entire year, once a month, we as-
sembled in his house.

Was your gymnasium coeducational?
No, it was only for boys, but I knew some girls through my sister.
Although she was a year and a half older than me, we were in the
same grade because, when the time had arrived to enroll her (she
was then six and a half), my parents thought: "The boy can go to
school too. Let's see how he will manage." I was five years old,
but had no problems, and thus we remained in the same grade.

Which were your favorite subjects?
I liked history and geography, but I was also rather good at math-
ematics.

And classics?
I did fairly well in Latin, but I liked Greek better. I realized that
it was a magnificent language, with a great literature; but four
years of study was not enough. The story of Oedipus and of other
Greek tragedies filled me with enthusiasm, but perhaps I was even
more taken by other things I read.

49

Who were the first authors you read with passion?
I read quite a bit of history. At that time it was quite fashionable
to read biographies — those by Emil Ludwig, for example — of
great historical personalities. I was very interested in the detail of
specific historical events. I loved *Buddenbrooks*, by Thomas Mann,
and the novels of Tolstoy and Dostoyevsky. I read all of Dostoyevsky's novels, obviously in German, and those I failed to read I
read later in France, still in German. I had become almost a Dostoyevsky expert.

*In the period when you began reading Marx and joined the socialist
youth movement, did you continue to like and read Dostoyevsky?*
Certainly. I had also begun to read a lot of Nietzsche, though I
was only sixteen years old at the time, and I asked myself insis-
tently: How can I reconcile Marx and Nietzsche?

*How did your family react to your decision to join the socialist youth
movement?*
Well, my parents were concerned by my decision to become a
socialist, but it was normal that they should have worried about
it. My sister and I had entered the phase where children are frequently in conflict with their parents, and we decided to travel
down our own road, in any event. On Sundays, we used to go to
the countryside in our blue shirts and red kerchiefs — and on those
occasions we might easily have encountered a gang of Nazis.

Did you ever run into such gangs? Did you ever provoke them?
No, only insults were exchanged.

And how did the meetings of the socialist youth groups take place?
We met once a week, in a place near the famous Sportpalast. We
would discuss our program, and sometimes we participated in

the meetings organized by the Social Democratic Party, for in-
stance on May Day.

On such occasions did you have meetings with workers?
We were supposed to be a workers' movement. In our group
there were, of course, many "bourgeois" elements. For example,
in our neighborhood there were many Mensheviks, or rather
children of Mensheviks, grown and raised in Germany, but children of Russians. I knew one of these Russians. He was rather
well known, his name was Raphael Rein; he was a prominent
Menshevik who had been a member of the Bund, which was the
Jewish Socialist Party of Poland. To be part of this party you had
to have a Jewish name; so, he chose the name of Abramovich. He
had spent some time in prison in czarist Russia, went into exile
in Vienna, returned to Russia, and then left for Berlin at the beginning of the 1920s, when it became impossible for the Mensheviks to continue living in the Soviet Union.

*Were there debates in your group about what was then occurring in
the social democratic movement?*
Certainly. That was exactly the moment when the socialist youth
groups split because of the *Tolerierungspolitik* — that is, because of
the party's policy of tolerating (or supporting) the government
of Chancellor Brüning. This split, I remember, took place precisely when Willy Brandt was a member of our group; he was my
age and we both belonged to the left wing of the party. But we
did not all agree on the advisability of a split, and some of us
decided to stay within the old group and not to join the new one,
the *Sozialistische Arbeiterpartei*, or the SAP. This was the first time
I experienced the conflict between "exit" and "voice," and I had
to choose whether to express my disagreement from within the
party or from without.

In any event, the socialist youth group was primarily a discussion group?

Yes, and I decided to stick with it, in order to retain some possibility of influencing the choices of the party.

On a more personal level — if the question isn't too indiscreet — did you have any important love affairs during this period?

No problem. I have some precise memories. During these years I had various amorous affairs, in connection with my political activity. (Our group had women too.) I remember in particular two girls with whom I had close relations during the Berlin period. One was the daughter of the Menshevik I mentioned before, the other came from a working-class family. This situation made the political activity even more pleasant.

What did you do together? Did you ever go dancing?

No, during that time, at most we marched together! Sometimes I would walk the girls home; these were moments where we were by ourselves, alone, but on the whole everything took place in a very spartan way!

Considering your relation with these children of Mensheviks, one wonders if you were informed at the time about what was then going on in the Soviet Union.

Certainly, we talked about it. The father of the girl I talked about before was a very committed Menshevik who wrote and worked against the Communist regime. We certainly knew something of what was going on in Russia; but the children are always more to the left than the parents, and we thought the situation in Russia was improving. This was the period of the first five-year plan, and we didn't know anything then about the horrors of the Soviet regime. We compared the Great Depression in the West with the reconstruction that was going forward in the Soviet Union, so that communism did not look so bad. Clearly, a lively discussion took place about these matters in our group, but our decision to stay within the social democratic party also hung together with the refusal to follow the rigid line that had been adopted everywhere within the Communist Party.

Did you have contact with the Communists?
No, at that time I didn't have direct contact with them, I didn't know them personally. Occasionally we would meet, during our weekend excursions, and then we would engage in political discussions.

At that time, did you read Marx and Marxist literature?
Yes, I read a lot of Marx, Lenin, Engels, Kautsky, and so on.

At that age, one usually has a very precise position on matters — for example, did you also read Rosa Luxemburg?
Yes, a little; I knew about the discussions between Luxemburg and Lenin. I was fascinated by Lenin. I liked his writings of 1917, which are full of tactical flexibility, and I think his influence can be noted in some parts of my work — for example, in *Journeys Toward Progress*, when I speak about how to carry out reforms in Latin America. The idea of "reform mongering" goes back in some way to my early readings of Lenin.

At that time did you write for newspapers or reviews?
No, I didn't write at all for publication. I was sixteen and I still had to graduate from high school. I graduated from the Französische Gymnasium in 1932, and then I did my first year of university in Berlin.

In what subject?
At that time I was still looking; I studied something between law
and economics. In my last year in Germany I was mostly occupied with political activity; at a certain point I came close to joining a group of Social Democrats which called itself *Neu Beginnen*,
or "New Start," and I noted that important members of the party
were part of it. Among them was my old friend Heinrich Ehrmann and a well-known political analyst by the name of Richard
Löwenthal, a kind of German Raymond Aron. In his writings,
which we read in the thirties in Paris, he formulated the first
serious analysis of national socialism, mainly because it marked
a departure from the orthodox Marxist versions, according to
which Nazism was merely a late version of capitalism. Löwenthal
wrote a series of important papers on this topic. He left Berlin
for Prague in 1933, then went to London.

*During the early months of 1933, was your group in any way pre-
pared for the events of that year?*
We realized that the Nazis had become very strong, but nobody
was prepared for what was going to happen. Even after Hinden-
burg had called on Hitler to form a new government, things did
not change fundamentally until the Reichstag fire, which really
marked the beginning of the political terror.

*In your youth groups did you talk about the possibility of organized
resistance, of taking up arms, or of clandestine opposition?*
After the Reichstag fire, all the opposition parties were simply
abolished; there was no longer any place where we could get together, and as a result we longer met. However, we continued to
have personal contact and decided to continue seeing each other
in our homes. Someone was able to get hold of a duplicating
machine, but we did not know where to put it, where to hide it.

We wanted to continue giving voice to our dissent and to publish a paper. That is when Eugenio Colorni intervened. We knew him because he had become very friendly with my sister Ursula.

So you knew each other in Berlin?
Yes, he noticed her in the university library and they got to know each other. When Hitler came to power, Colorni told us that we could use his hotel room, because as a foreigner he was not suspected. Thus we came to print our publications and flyers there.

At that time, what did you think when comparing German and Italian fascism?
To tell the truth, we knew rather little about Italian fascism. We knew that it wanted the end of democracy. For us "fascism" was just an ugly word that we used as a *Schimpfwort*, an insult. The worst thing the Communists did was to call Social Democrats "social fascists" — this was absolutely the worst thing imaginable to say about your enemies.

Did Colorni speak to you about Italy?
At that time Colorni was Ursula's friend, and I didn't see much of him. We didn't have much occasion to talk. I left just a little later for Paris, at the beginning of April 1933.

And Ursula?
She left three months later, also for Paris. There, I tried to earn some money, mainly by giving German lessons. There was in particular a French family to whom I taught German who later invited me to spend the summer at their place in Normandy. By that time it was July, and Ursula, who had fled from Germany, came to join us briefly.

And your parents?

My father had died suddenly in March. My mother remained in Berlin for many years, with my younger sister, and didn't leave until 1939 (my sister left in 1938).

You said before that your parents were worried by your political militancy. Was this merely the understandable fear of any parent or was it also specifically due to your parents' worries about Nazi anti-Semitism? In other words, when did the fact that you were Jewish become the principal problem?

My parents were obviously quite conscious of the problem of anti-Semitism. My father was a very reflective person, but he was not particularly decisive. On this matter I recall an amusing anecdote: When I was about thirteen, I talked to my father and in due course asked him a question to which he admitted not having an answer. I remember running to my sister's room to tell her, much surprised, "You know what? Vati doesn't have a Weltanschauung!" I still remember the readings my father and I did together. During a certain period I was much taken by the Austro-Marxists I was reading. I showed some particular passage to my father, who was very struck by it. So his mind was quite open. On the other hand, my mother was a more downright type; she was very clear about what she liked and disliked.

And how did you arrive at the decision to emigrate?

At some point I simply decided to leave. It was largely my decision, even though I talked about it with some friends.

And Ursula?

Ursula was more involved with certain groups of people — by May or June 1933 many of her friends had been arrested and sent to concentration camps. Then, at a certain point, she too decided to leave and did so with others. I, on the other hand, left by myself.

Weren't you afraid that there might be consequences for your mother?
No, at that time many people left the country: in a way, that is what the Nazis wanted.

So, after one year at the university in Berlin, you left for Paris and enrolled at a university there?
That is more or less correct. Once I was in Paris I tried to figure out how I could continue my studies. I have described this matter in a talk I gave in Paris when I spoke at the Ecole des Sciences Politiques on the occasion of an honorary degree I was awarded there in 1988. It is a curious story, which I recount in *A Propensity to Self-Subversion* [chap. 8]. In it I tell how, in Paris in 1933, I got to know Michel Debré, then a student at the Ecole, who advised me strongly against trying to get into that school because, as he said, "You are a refugee, you can *never* become a diplomat or a civil servant," and that "Sciences Po" led exclusively to that sort of career.

So what did you choose?
I chose another of those *grandes écoles*, the Ecole des Hautes Etudes Commerciales, and I spent two years there.

You studied mostly economics?
Economics, but also finance, accounting, and so on.

Were you comfortable in Paris right away?
Yes, I became close to the French; I had a head start, given my knowledge of the language. I really took to life in Paris and I became friendly with the family to whom I gave German lessons.

Where did you live?
At first, I shared an apartment with my sister in the 15th arron-
dissement, where many refugees lived, and later went to stay in
the Cité Universitaire, where I had a single room.

How long did you stay in Paris?
The first time, I lived there from 1933 to 1935, then I stayed in
London from 1935 to 1936. In the summer of 1935 I went briefly
to Forte dei Marmi in Italy, because Colorni, who had become
engaged to my sister, had a house there. I returned to Italy in
December for Ursula and Eugenio's marriage. Incidentally, I just
finished reading the fine book by Clara Sereni, *Il Gioco dei regni*,
in which she tells a story about the day before Eugenio's wed-
ding. He had to make sure that his Communist cousin (and Clara's
father) Emilio Sereni (whose surname was Mimmo) left Italy for
Paris — illegally, of course. That evening, during the rehearsal
dinner, Eugenio took me aside and said, "You have to accompany
me to Central Station. We can pretend that we are observing the
old custom of 'burying the celibate's life.'" So we left the dinner
to go to the station. Once we'd arrived there Eugenio asked me
to wait for him and to notify certain people if he didn't return.
Eugenio had to make sure that Mimmo Sereni was on the train
and that everything was going well. After we had made sure that
everything was in good order, the two of us went back to the
family dinner!

Were you already in contact with the Italian Resistance in Paris?
No, in Paris I only had contacts with German émigrés. But I soon
got tired of this group and realized that I wanted to study seriously and decide what to do with my life.

During this time who were your principal teachers?
When I was receiving another honorary degree, this time in Nanterre, in economics, I mentioned that I had had some excellent teachers in economic geography, and in money and banking, such as Albert Demangeon and Henry Pommery.

But the most important year for your professional formation was the one you spent at the London School of Economics?
Yes, in 1935 I received a fellowship for a year at that school. To understand my intellectual formation it is important to understand what was then happening in modern economics. For me this was a decisive year, even though the London School was not at all Keynesian. It was rather anti-Keynesian — in fact, Lionel Robbins and Friedrich von Hayek were among its principal teachers. I took some of their courses. But there were also some younger people, about my age, who had fled from Germany or Hungary. I joined these people spontaneously and we formed a group. They were all Keynesian and had been to Cambridge to hear the master. Among them there was a brilliant young economist, already well-known, by the name of Abba Lerner, and some excellent teachers of international trade.

Did you also go to Cambridge?
Yes, to meet Piero Sraffa, who was, I think, a cousin of Colorni's. Eugenio wrote me a letter of introduction, so I managed to have a long and agreeable talk with Sraffa, who was then totally absorbed by his edition of the works of David Ricardo.

What were you working on while you were at the London School?
I didn't follow a regular plan of studies, since I already had my French diploma. I decided to study for my own account — in particular, a special problem of recent French economic history: the

economic reform of 1925–26 and the history of the "franc Poincaré." At the time, this was an important topic for the French, and since I had lived in France and was convinced I would return there, I decided to study some problems of recent French economic history. I started a research project in this field under the supervision of Professor Barrett Whale, a fine teacher in international economics at the London School. This was in effect the project I developed later in my dissertation in Trieste.

But in Trieste you followed a course of specialization or some other course in view of the doctorate?
At Trieste, through the system of equivalences, I received credit for the examinations I had already taken in Paris. I had to pass certain examinations in such subjects as commercial law, so I did take some courses. But principally I had to write my thesis: I did it by finishing the work I had started in London, reworking it and translating it into Italian.

So, this is when you learned Italian?
As soon as I knew there was a good chance that I would go and live in Italy, I took Italian lessons in Paris from an antifascist refugee named Renzo Giua, who later died in the Spanish Civil War. My sister has written a beautiful portrait of him in her book.

And Eugenio Colorni, what did he do then? Did he teach at the university?
No, he never taught at the university, because he refused to swear loyalty to the Fascist regime. He was a teacher in an institute for teachers and taught philosophy.

Did you go to Italy essentially because Ursula and Eugenio were there?
In part that was my motivation, but there were other reasons.
When I returned from London to Paris, I had financial problems:
I had no work. Also, before I went to Italy in 1936, I had gone
to Spain. After London I stopped for several weeks in Paris, where
I learned about the outbreak of the Spanish Civil War — so I de-
cided to go to Spain.

*Now you say that you simply decided to leave for the Spanish Civil
War, but a short time ago you told us that you were passing through a
period of indifference to refugees and refugee politics and that you
had decided to concentrate on your studies. Was it Spain that pushed
you into renewed political commitment?*
Yes, you're right, I did want to study, but at the same time I realized that fascism was advancing and that I could not just sit and
look on without doing anything. So, when I felt that there was
the possibility of doing something I seized the opportunity.

*And how did it work? Did you join one of the brigades, or did you go
on your own account?*
I went by myself, directly to Barcelona. There I joined a mixed
group — Italians, Germans, and French — who were given a bit of
training, but politically the group was quickly taken over by the
Communists.

And what was your reaction?
I still considered myself a Socialist, but in Catalonia the Socialist
Party came quickly under Communist control. I had the names
of some people connected with the POUM (Partido Obrero de
Unificación Marxista), through my Menshevik friends of Paris,
particularly through the son of Abramovich, who was a close
friend. His name was Mark Rein and he was the elder brother of

the girl I had been friendly with in Berlin. Later, Mark Rein went to Barcelona himself to help the Republic as an engineer. He disappeared rapidly and almost certainly was killed by the Stalinists. In this period Stalin tried to hit his principal enemies by killing their sons: he had already killed one of Trotsky's sons and now was trying to do the same with Abramovich's son. We found out about this only later in Trieste.

How long were you at the front?
Two to three months. After having returned to Barcelona, we were supposed to join the international brigades in Madrid, but I decided not to go.

Why?
Because by now the formation was entirely under Communist control. Moreover, some of the Italians I met told me that my presence would be more useful in Italy, if I would support my brother-in-law's antifascist activities there.

So was this the turning point that led you to become a full-time militant in Italy? You went to Italy for a kind of political mission...
This is correct, but only in part. My brother-in-law, for example, was not just a committed antifascist, he was also an active teacher. In sum, there was no need for us to become "professional revolutionaries." We were antifascists, but in a way this was a collateral activity of ours.

When you were in Spain did you get any military instruction?
Yes, we were given a training course, even though it was quite elementary.

Who did you meet at the front, any Italians?
A few. Some of them knew Eugenio Colorni well, but he had remained in Italy. Later, Renzo Giua came from France to Spain, but we didn't see each other there.

And after Spain?
Afterward, the strange thing was that I had a German passport in good order, issued two years before, without any stamp indicating that I had entered Spain or that I had left it! Taking the train from Barcelona along the Mediterranean, I traveled straight to Trieste and stayed there for a while with Ursula and Eugenio. Eugenio attempted to find me a job at the university and actually arranged for me to become an assistant in statistics, with Professor Luzzatto-Fegiz, a well-known demographer. From then on, I made frequent trips, from Trieste to Paris and back, to communicate with Mimmo Sereni and Angelo Tasca, who at the time had become quite friendly with Eugenio. Yes, it was fun, this going back and forth, passing from Catalonia to Fascist Italy, and from there to Paris and then again to Italy, all of this seemingly under the nose of the Fascists!

Let me return for a moment to my contacts with the POUM. We were quite pessimistic at the time about the possibility of maintaining an independent Socialist Party, considering that the Stalinists had assumed the dominant position on the left.

When you were in Spain, the conflict between the Communists and the other groups in Catalonia was already in the open, the various murders and betrayals had already started?
Yes, at the time I perhaps failed to realize how terrible the situation really was, up to what point these cruelties had progressed.

But when you had these various contacts in Paris — Giorgio Amendola speaks about it in his memoirs — you were in contact with various antifascist groups, including the Communists?
Yes, because there were personal ties. As his daughter Clara notes in her book, Mimmo had troubles with the Communists precisely because of his contacts with the "dubious" ones. Actually, we were involved with these contacts because we knew Mark Rein's mother well. She was a very nervous person, psychologically unstable; after the disappearance of her son she suffered a breakdown. When we learned about that in Trieste in April of 1937, Ursula asked a "courier" of ours to go to Paris to bring some flowers to her. He did, and from there he went straight away to see Mimmo. Later, when Mimmo went to Moscow, he was interrogated about his contact with Abramovich, that "dangerous enemy" of the Soviet Union. The facts seemed to be replete with evidence that Mimmo had contacts which, in the eyes of the Stalinists, constituted one of the worst crimes. All of this had, however, happened as a result of pure coincidence.

You obviously were in quite close contact with Colorni during your stay in Italy. What was his position in the antifascist struggle?
Colorni was the head of the "internal center," or the Socialist Party. Obviously he did not tell me everything. He used quite a bit of discretion. He always tried to unite the various factions of antifascism without giving special privileges to one in particular. At first he had been a member of the group Giustizia e Libertà, but then he had become a Socialist. He had simultaneously maintained good relations with the "Justice and Liberty" group with whom he became quite close after the Rosellis were murdered. He had some contacts with all the components of antifascism. My contacts in Paris were also multiple. I often saw Tasca who had in the meantime become a determined anticommunist.

64

How did you manage to have relations with Sereni and Tasca at the same time?

I am not sure I had these relations at the same time and during the same trip; I made several trips. During one of them I received a double-bottom suitcase, or rather a double-top one, from Mimmo Sereni. This was something quite different from a double-bottom suitcase, and it was a real innovation. I carried several messages to Tasca. With Mimmo my relations came to be limited to an exchange of information and some instructions, whereas my relations with Tasca were more open. One day I also met Nicola Chiaromonte and Mario Levi, who were both working with him. Mario Levi was the brother of Natalia Ginzburg, the writer.

So one could say that Sereni was a person of few words who issued directives, whereas Tasca, Chiaromonte, and Levi were more inclined to discussions?

That is about right. When I returned to Paris in 1938, I saw the latter rather frequently.

A statement that struck me in Ursula's memoirs is that she felt the Italian atmosphere was "freer."

Let me try to explain. In the first place, in Paris, the refugees always asked themselves, Where do I really belong in the struggle against the Nazis? — and there were many intrigues around that question. That is why I withdrew from any political contacts when I returned from Italy to Paris, and I kept aloof from the émigrés. Of course I maintained some friendships, for example, those with the Mensheviks. At that point, I got to know some French intellectuals, such as Robert Marjolin and Raymond Aron, an admirable group, and I worked as an economist with a specialty in Italian economic affairs. This was the life I led in the last year of my life in France, before the war broke out. Let me go back, however, to Ursula's observation. In it there was a certain critique of the Italian lifestyle. In her book there is a fine chapter entitled "I Am Becoming an Italian Lady": she was becoming a real Italian housewife, and in this sense she felt that she was about to lose her independence and to depend too much on a series of commodities and comforts of daily life, comforts that she had never experienced before, either in Germany or France. This was also the first time she had a house of her own and she began to have children.

When you stayed in Italy, did you travel a lot within the country, with contacts in other cities?
No, not really. I stayed in Trieste, was wholly absorbed by my job as a university assistant, and worked a lot on some ideas I started to develop. My work at the time was mostly centered on demography, one of my real passions. I wrote some articles in this field, published one of them in the *Giornale degli Economisti*, and was unable to publish another one, which went against the demographic policy of Mussolini.

How did you develop this interest in Italian demography?
Because the Fascist regime, to promote its natalist policy, helped to publish many statistical data and studies in this field which had never been published before: for example, on the fecundity of the Italian woman according to the number of children that have been conceived or have survived, and so on. This was quite interesting data. I based an article on it in which I demonstrated that the official policy could have counterproductive results: for example, when you had six children there would be four survivors, but when you had seven children there might only be three survivors. Therefore I asserted in the article that even from the point of view of a natalist policy it was absurd to give prizes

to women who give birth to all these children! I thought it was a good argument and still think it is, but I did not succeed in getting it published. Perhaps I shall publish it posthumously.

Did you also study philosophy, in addition to economics, statistics, and similar fields?
No. I certainly read some philosophy, under the influence of my brother-in-law, but this was hardly my main interest.

Did you consider yourself a Marxist, in 1936–37?
I think I began to have some doubts in this regard. A very fine German writer, Hans Sahl, whom I met in Marseilles in 1940, who died recently in Germany at the age of ninety, wrote in his memoirs that people moved away from communism during the thirties in three phases: they started questioning Stalin, then Lenin, and finally they doubted even Marx. In his autobiography Sahl says: When I lived in Paris, in the thirties, I was full of admiration for Silone, who was also living in Paris at that time. So I called him and realized that Silone was already at the second or third stage of this process while I was still stuck in the first one!

When you read Marx, what impressed you most about his thought?
The Eighteenth Brumaire of Louis Bonaparte was a particularly fine work. His historical books were much less orthodox than his economic ones.

And political ethics?
In general, I have never had much interest in ethics, in contrast to Michael Walzer, whose office is located right here next to my own. Perhaps we get along so well because we are interested in different things! I like to understand how things happen, how change actually takes place.

So you read Marx's historical works, The Communist Manifesto,
Class Struggles in France...
Yes, and I read *Capital.* I also read quite a bit of Engels. For
example, his *Anti-Dühring* impressed me a great deal.

In 1938 you left Italy. Was that because of Mussolini's new racial laws?
Exactly. I was in contact with a famous demographer and economist, Giorgio Mortara, who was the director of the *Giornale degli
Economisti* in Milan; he had published my first article and later
advised against publishing the second one. I recall that I asked his
advice on whether to stay in Italy when the first racial laws were
passed. He answered with a beautiful letter telling me "much
time will be needed before this obsession, this cholera" — that
was the metaphor he used — "will be spent." He advised me to
leave. At this point, Ursula, Eugenio, and I went for a brief vacation to Selva di Val Gardena in the Dolomites. It was July, and
immediately afterward I left for Paris. Eugenio was arrested with
a great deal of fanfare as soon as he returned to Trieste. This
would certainly have happened to me too, as I was denounced in
the Fascist press as a collaborator with Eugenio and as a German
Jew.

Ursula, though, remained in Trieste?
Yes, she did and was not persecuted. This is an example of how
fascism was less inhuman than Nazism. When Eugenio was ban-
ished to the island of Ventotene, Ursula asked to be allowed to
follow him. In general this was not permitted, but the police
argued that "this poor foreign lady must be allowed to rejoin her
husband," so she was allowed to go.

At that time, they already had a daughter.
Yes, Silvia, and I believe Ursula was already pregnant with another daughter, Renata, who was born in 1939. Eugenio was arrested in 1938.

What were your first contacts with the United States?
I had none until I worked for the organization of clandestine expatriation that was set up by Varian Fry in Marseilles in 1940. By the way, a new edition of his book *Assignment: Rescue* has recently been published, with an introduction by me.

That book was first published in 1944?
Yes, under the title *Surrender on Demand*. Now, however, in conjunction with the new Museum of the Holocaust in Washington, a new edition appeared, sponsored by the museum. At the same time, the museum organized a special exhibition on the Varian Fry story, and I was asked to contribute certain documents of mine, such as my false identity cards and other fake documents I carried.

Let's talk a little about this "rescue operation." When you were leaving Italy to go back to France, you carried only a German passport?
Yes, that was all I had.

And the experience with the Emergency Rescue Committee?
That all followed my voluntary engagement into the French Army after World War II broke out in 1939. The opportunity to enter the army had been created by the Daladier government, after the Munich Agreement of 1938. Up to that time, the only way for foreigners to enlist in the French Army was by way of the Foreign Legion. This was not truly the ideal choice for all. So, the French government decided to make it possible for for-

eigners to enlist by opening up a list for those who in case of war would want to fight for France during the duration of the war. Accordingly I signed myself up after the Munich Treaty, and it so happened that precisely on September 1, 1939, the day the war broke out, I was called up for basic training. I found myself joining a group of German and Italian volunteers, and we formed a company which spent the "phony war" period in a zone west of Paris near Le Mans. But in April the German offensive started, and soon enough we were surrounded. At this point, it became clear that we ran the risk of being taken prisoner by the Germans.

Up to that point you had spent about seven months in the French Army?
Yes, but it was not wholly a period of idleness. We were kept quite busy building a new rail link to a munitions factory. We were being used as workers. The name of our company was in fact *bataillon d'ouvriers d'artillerie* (B.O.A.). When the Germans came uncomfortably close, a friend and I managed to convince our commanding officer, obviously a Frenchman, that we would be safer with French documents. With our German and Italian documents we risked being shot as traitors. So one night we got together and everyone chose his own new identity. The pretext was that we had lost our military papers "during the campaign" and that we needed a new document from the current military command. Thus, each of us had to invent a new identity. I changed my name to "Albert Hermant, né à Philadelphie."

And all this was done with the complicity of the commanding officer?
Yes, he was very understanding. He fully realized the serious danger we were exposed to. Of course, many would never have done what he did. The next day, the Germans were everywhere. I went by bicycle toward Bordeaux, and on the road I encountered

some German soldiers, who told me to go to the closest prisoners' camp. Because they were trying to reach the Spanish border,
they didn't have time to take me there. Instead of following those
orders I decided to escape from the zone that the Germans had
penetrated and flee to what was to become the "unoccupied
zone" of Vichy France. I went to Nîmes, in the south of France,
where I had some friends, and there I succeeded in getting my
demobilization from the French Army. Now I had to obtain new
civilian papers. In lieu of a birth certificate, which is normally
required, I found out it was possible to get hold of a *certificat
de vie* in which the mayor simply declares that "Mr. Hermant is
alive, considering the fact that he has presented himself physi-
cally in front of us."

At that point, I thought that I would spend the rest of the
war in this area, perhaps with these friends in Nîmes; but then
I became aware of Marseilles, of the people who were getting
together there, and of the possibility of getting out of France this
way. So I left for Marseilles, and one of the first people I met was
Varian Fry, who had just arrived with the mission to help a number of antinazi and antifascist refugees who were most at risk, to
get out of France. Fry had been sent to Europe by a committee
that had been formed by trade unions and by some professors of
the New School of Social Research, who were political refugees
— among the Italians, a prominent one was Max Ascoli. There
were quite a few French and Germans who were fully aware of
the risks run by people after the armistice signed by France and
Germany. One of the articles of the armistice committed the
French government to extradite any foreign national requested by
Germany. In southern France there were many well-known German refugees such as Rudolf Hilferding, Heinrich Mann, Rudolf
Breitscheid, and others. Fry arrived in France thinking that he
would be able to accomplish his mission in a short time; but he

remained there for over a year and was finally expelled from the country. I became a close collaborator of his; the whole story is very well told in his book *Surrender on Demand*, which I already mentioned.

You also went to Spain while this operation was taking place in the Pyrenees?
Yes, I tried to think of various ways to get people out. The main problem was to obtain the visas for some overseas destination (United States, Brazil, China) and then to get hold of a transit visa for Spain and Portugal since it was impossible to get a visa to get out of France — a *visa de sortie* — we were blocked in France. It was therefore necessary to leave France illegally and to enter Spain legally as soon as possible — otherwise one might be considered illegal immigrants. Unfortunately, some of our people got lost and were arrested in Spain. Franco Venturi, the Italian historian, suffered this fate. He was sent back to Italy by General Franco and spent the rest of the war in jail. I explored various ways of getting across the border in various alternative fashions. One of these routes was supposed to pass through Toulouse, but it did not work too well. In the end, the route via the Mediterranean was most reliable. Besides that, Fry gave me various tasks: I was supposed to get false visas from China and got involved in exchanging foreign currencies. Finally, the police started to investigate me on account of various illegal activities. I recall that one evening when I returned from a trip, Varian told me that the police had been looking for me. He advised me not even to return to my hotel and to leave the country right away. So I sent someone to collect my stuff at the hotel, and I left France for Spain and Portugal, by the Mediterranean route. It was December 1940.

Among the fleeing intellectuals who were you able to help?
A large number. I worked with Fry for six months, but he continued to carry on this activity for a while and in the end there were about two thousand people who were able to emigrate. Among them there were Hannah Arendt and her husband, Heinrich Blücher, whom I had known for a time: he had courted Ursula some time ago and we had been quite friendly.

Did you maintain any of these ties afterward?
Strangely enough, not very much. Later, I became more of a professional economist, I traveled a lot and did not see the "old crowd" any more. I remember, however, that one day — it was 1958 and I was teaching at Columbia University — I was walking on Columbus Avenue and saw someone who seemed familiar: it was my old friend from the thirties, Heinrich Blücher.

How was the Emergency Rescue Committee organized?
There were several phases. At the start, Fry directed the organization from his hotel room; then so many people came that we decided to open an office to permit us to offer relief to the many people who had no means whatsoever.

We analyzed in detail the material situation of the people who came to see us, but also looked at them from the point of view of the danger they were in. The problem was of course that the committee couldn't take care of all the emergency situations, nor could it get visas for everyone. Later, the committee was criticized for its alleged elitist character, for only helping the people who were somehow outstanding. In fact, though, the people who were outstanding were also those who ran the most risk at that point.

Part Two
The American Years

So, *in December 1940, you left Europe for America.*
Yes, I decided the time had come for me to leave too. I left with
two other people, one of whom I discovered to have been an old
friend and colleague of my father's in Berlin; I had not seen him
since then. My destination was Berkeley, California. During the
year prior to the war I had worked in Paris with an economist
from New Zealand, Jack Condliffe, who had been quite prominent at the League of Nations in Geneva. I had participated in a
research project of his on exchange control in various countries
and, because in France I had become something of an expert on
the Italian economy, I worked on the Italian part of the project.
Condliffe had formed a good opinion of me and my work. When
he learned that I was in Marseilles in a difficult situation, he managed to get me a research fellowship from the Rockefeller Foundation, which made it possible for me to obtain an American visa.
One of my tasks at the Fry committee was to be in contact with
the American consul and to keep track of any newly available
visas for entry into the United States. One day the consul said to
me, "I have here a new visa, for a certain Albert Hirschmann, do
you know him?" I replied, "Yes, I do seem to know him," and
explained to the consul the story about the mutation from
Hirschmann to Hermant. The consul told me that he was willing
to believe my story, but that he needed some proof. I had kept my
birth certificate in a trunk, along with a lot of other belongings, in
my hotel in Paris. At that point, it was impossible for me to
return. But there were people at the time who, for a fee, would go
to Paris to obtain documents. I paid, received my document, and
was able to get the visa.

Condliffe, the New Zealand economist, had in the meantime been promoted to professor of international economics at Berkeley. He was then directing a big research project, which I then joined. He was a real gentleman and asked me only to develop quite freely my own ideas in the field of political economy. Another person who worked with us was Alexander Gerschenkron, whose earlier work had been conducted in Russia and Austria. We worked in the same office. At this time he was writing *Bread and Democracy in Germany,* while I was writing my first book, *National Power and the Structure of Foreign Trade.*

When did you join the American army?
Two years later. I arrived in January 1941 and joined the army in March 1943.

And when did you acquire American citizenship?
During my military service. That is when I became Albert Hirschman, with just one *n.*

What pushed you to enlist?
It was the only thing foreigners were able to do at the time, if they did not want to abandon their liberty.

When you left for the army, were you already married?
Yes. I spent my first two years in America as an ordinary immigrant. During this time, I met Sarah in Berkeley and we were married very soon after, in June 1941. I was twenty-six years old and she twenty. She still had to finish her undergraduate studies. I joined the army in 1943, and when I was about to be sent overseas, to North Africa, we decided to have a child. Sarah came to live with me in Washington, where our first child, Katia, was conceived. She was born in Los Angeles in 1944. In April 1943, I

75

left for overseas and remained abroad almost two years. My other daughter, Lisa, was born later, in 1946.

Where were you sent, to which front?
I was sent first to North Africa and then to Italy. In Algiers I met a group of Italian antifascists and French intellectuals. Among the latter was the wife of Albert Camus, whose books *The Stranger* and *The Myth of Sisyphus* I had read recently and liked very much. His wife made me very happy by telling me that I resembled her husband! In Italy, I served in the Office of Strategic Services (OSS) and was in touch with partisans who were behind the lines.

Did you succeed in keeping in touch with Ursula during this period?
No, or rather I received letters from time to time, quite rarely. She and Eugenio were transferred from the island of Ventotene to the mainland, at Melfi. Then the Badoglio government took over, and they were able to leave Melfi. Later, in 1944, I heard about Eugenio's death. I was then in Algiers and learned the news from the group of Italian antifascists I had met. For me it was a terrible blow. I realized that he was the person who had counted most in my life. Ursula left for Switzerland with Altiero later in the year.

At the end of the war, were you still in Europe?
Yes, I remained there until the end of 1945. I was now in a counterespionage unit, and there were many things to accomplish after the end of the war. For example, I worked as an interpreter during the trial of a German general, one of the first trials of a war criminal. He had ordered the shooting of some American soldiers in uniform who had been captured by the Germans. This was in contravention of the Geneva Convention on Prisoners of War. The trial took place in Rome. After the end of the war

in Europe, I stayed another six months in Rome. During this period, I was able to see Ursula and her children frequently. I remember that I often rode through the city in my jeep, feeling like the happy American soldier.

You went around with those famous American candy bars?
Yes, here I am, I still have the photos of Ursula's children, sitting inside the large Camel cigarette cartons!

What was your rank?
Very low, I was a simple sergeant.

Your wife was in the States while you were in Europe. Were you sure you wanted to go on living in America?
I saw this as the only sensible decision. Obviously, everything was possible: Germany, France, Italy. But by now I was an American citizen. I had a family, a wife, a daughter there, and I had started a career in the United States, where I had just published my first book, receiving the first recognition for my activity as an economist. Moreover, the United States was at that moment really a superpower: in my life I had suffered so many defeats that I was only too glad to be on the side of the victors for once!

In 1946 you were given an important job at the Federal Reserve Board. In connection with this work, there was the expectation of strong ties with Italy and France . . .
This is correct. It so happened that Gerschenkron was already at the Federal Reserve Board, and he invited me to join him. The first article on which I worked was about the means of reconstruction that were used in France and Italy, respectively. I tried hard to be a technical economist, for a change. I had frequent contacts with Egidio Ortona, who was then economic adviser at

the Italian embassy, and with Pierre Ledoux, who had the same position at the French embassy and who had been in my class at the Ecole des Hautes Etudes Commerciales in 1933–35.

At that time, what was the general attitude toward the Marshall Plan? There is no doubt that the Marshall Plan was a great invention. In part because I was convinced of that, I decided to return to the United States at the end of the war. I was very well disposed toward United States postwar economic policy and greatly admired the people who were involved in the elaboration and the management of the Marshall Plan. Their political and economic plans seemed to me to be carried forward with much intelligence and in new, previously untried forms. I liked the concept of "large-scale grant giving"; this was an original idea, as was later underlined by a French intellectual of the period, Georges Bataille, in his book *The Accursed Share*. It represented the invention of a new type of cooperative relationship between nations, a relationship that became possible because of the Soviet threat. But this threat was not the original motivation. The most profound reason for the Marshall Plan was the desire to strengthen European democracy, in addition to the equally important idea of contributing to the process of European unification. The United States applied a great deal of pressure on Europe to elaborate a common policy. In this way, Altiero Spinelli and I worked together on various occasions. A close collaboration resulted at times, particularly when he came to this country and I put him in touch with various people.

For you who worked on the Marshall Plan, was it more important to work through the national governments or to achieve results through direct action?
My influence was of course limited, because as an economist I was not involved in top political affairs. Nevertheless, I exercised a certain influence as a member of different interagency committees. I was particularly involved in matters involving France and Italy and later, around 1950, in the organization of the European Payments Union (EPU). Moreover, I was a member of a kind of "brain trust" that worked on new initiatives within the Marshall Plan agency.

Was Gerschenkron a member?
No, he had gone to teach at Harvard in 1948. Besides, his principal concern at that point was the Soviet Union. As for myself, I specialized in France and Italy and had direct contacts with their governments. I wrote a rather well-known article, "Inflation and Deflation in Italy," which dealt with the successful anti-inflationary policy of Einaudi, then director of the Bank of Italy. For it I received special recognition from the bank. Later Luigi Einaudi became president of Italy whereas, at the bank, Paolo Baffi and Donato Menichella were close friends of mine and important policy makers. In France, I also had good relations with the government. It was quite a special experience for me to have so much power, as representative of a superpower, after having been a refugee for many years. Suddenly it was up to me to tell them how to handle their monetary policy!

Did you live in Washington during this period?
Yes, from 1946 to 1952.

How did you end up in Colombia afterward?
I went there in 1952. In Washington I increasingly had the feeling that the problems were a bit tired. The controversy over the
European Payments Union seemed to go on and on; our secretary of the treasury was very much against it. In our group, on the
contrary, we were in favor of European unity, and we were for
the United States contributing funds to the European Payments
Union, which eventually happened later. A considerable polemic
occurred within the government, and I understood little by little
how public policies were resolved in this country. This type of
conflict did not seem to go away, and at a certain point I got tired
of circling around the same problems. In the meantime, my
interests had shifted to other areas to which I had not devoted
sufficient attention, such as the problem of development in the
"backward" countries. In 1952, the possibility of either going to
Europe — always in connection with the European Payments
Union — or of going to Colombia as an economic adviser arose. I
opted to take the second road, because it was new. At that point
my wife thought I had gone mad: she wanted to return to Paris,
where, after all, she had lived most of her youth. But after a short
time she was quite satisfied with my choice.

What did your wife do in Colombia?
She did not work, she was quite occupied with the house. Our
children were small, the house was big, we had two or three
domestics. She led the typical life of the "señora" and learned
how to speak Spanish and be comfortable in the "ambiente."

Did you have problems with the Committee on Un-American Activities?
None at all.

And in Colombia, how did you organize your work?

It was not easy. It was a strange situation, and it took time to understand it. There was a new planning council that had been established on the recommendation of the World Bank, which had sent a mission to the country. But the Colombians said, "If you want us to set up a new planning council, send us an economist who is capable of advising us." The Bank looked around, my name was mentioned, and I was ready to come — and in fact did come. I was never an employee of the World Bank, but entered into a direct contract with the Colombian government, for two years. At the end of these two years, I did not renew the contract, but decided to stay in Colombia. These two years had been quite tiring. We had General Rojas Pinilla's coup, among other things. I felt a bit frustrated. In addition, we had conflicts with other American consultants who had joined us, especially with one, Lauchlin Currie, a Canadian who had been part of Roosevelt's "brain trust" and was a man of considerable intelligence. He was the leader of the first mission of the World Bank in Colombia and he also decided to stay in Colombia. He did have problems with the Committee on Un-American Activities, was accused of being a Communist, and decided not to return to the United States. He died in Colombia when he was over ninety. The World Bank sent another person to Colombia who in my opinion had too rigid a view about how to organize planning. He gave me some ideas how not to plan! In spite of these problems, I was making some good contacts and my work was appreciated by many people.

Hence, when I had served my two years in Colombia, I decided to stay in Bogotá and open my own consulting office, with the following title: "Albert Hirschman, economic and financial adviser." I worked a great deal, at the beginning for firms and banks and for publicly owned utilities that were trying to obtain financing and loans from the World Bank. Later we began to do market studies for private firms. I had a partner and a few employees. Then one day I received an invitation to participate in a conference organized by the Massachusetts Institute of Technology in Cambridge. Max Millikan and Walt Rostow were there, along with many other "experts." I presented a report on economic development which aroused much interest. People started to pay attention to me. Two years later I received a letter in which I was invited to spend a full year at Yale University so as to write about my experience. My friends from the Marshall Plan period had by then almost all become university professors. (Quite a few of them were now at Yale, and they tried to save me from the "tropics.") I accepted the Yale offer with the idea of returning to Colombia the next year, as I still had quite a few contracts pending there. But then I remained at Yale another year to finish writing *The Strategy of Economic Development*. By then my daughters needed to decide which high school to enroll in, and I began to receive proposals from various universities. Finally, I received an interesting offer from Columbia University, which I accepted.

So you first went to Columbia, then to Harvard, and finally to Princeton's Institute for Advanced Study?
Exactly.

Let's take a small step backward and talk about your experience of daily life in Latin America.
I enjoyed my life there and found the people with whom I worked rather intelligent. I made new friendships. I met a group of people that had new ideas about cooperation between private firms and public entities. At one time I was actively involved in the attempt to develop a regional authority on the model of the

Tennessee Valley Authority. The idea to create a multifunctional entity was then quite widespread. This entity would provide irrigation, electric power, and even land reform. This kind of work gave me the desire to begin to know in depth the reality of this country, and it put me into contact with many people. Now it hardly ever happened that I would take a plane without meeting this or that minister or corporate executive whom I knew personally. I felt positive about all this because I had the feeling that the country was moving forward. However, I don't want to deny the tremendous problems the country was going through — we must not forget that a civil war was still going on — but in any event we had the perception that the country was progressing.

When you returned to the United States in 1956, did that interrupt your relations with Latin America?
No, not at all. When I lived in Colombia I traveled little, except to get to know the country itself. Outside, I had only been to Ecuador and Venezuela. At a certain point, when I started my consulting business, the U.S. Department of Commerce asked me to write a manual on Central America. On that occasion, I visited various countries in the area, passing two to three weeks in each to talk to people and to collect materials. Then I returned to Bogotá to write the book. Perhaps in the end it wasn't a very deep work, but when I returned to the States I was probably the economist who had spent the most time in that part of the Continent and knew it best. I became famous because, with the Cuban Revolution, and the subsequent explosion of interest in that country, I became one of the most sought after "experts." I was even asked to join President Kennedy's staff, but I was then writing another book and didn't want to interrupt that process.

What did you think of Cuba? What was your attitude toward the revolution?

My attitude was at first very positive. I did not know that country through direct experience, I had never been there. But I knew the president of the Central Bank of Cuba, Felipe Pazos, who originally was on Fidel's side. But this relationship lasted only a brief time; he was forced to leave after as little as a year. Soon I had doubts about the correctness of the Cuban political line and about the enthusiasm with which Fidel Castro embraced the Soviet model. Fidel visited New York and Columbia University, and we had a discussion with him and others, but it was not interesting.

My theoretical work in those years dealt with the question of how the United States could play a positive role in Latin America, what possibilities there were to promote certain reforms. This was the point of view from which I undertook to write my second book on the theme of development, to be called *Journeys Toward Progress*. In my opinion, the American vision here was too simple-minded, and our proposals were excessively categorical and a priori.

From the beginning, you and the World Bank entertained very different views here, didn't you?

Yes, I dissented from the Bank in matters of planning, because I thought it was unreasonable in practical terms. But then, in 1959, once the Cuban revolution had broken out, many people thought that the only way to prevent other revolutions was to undertake large-scale reform policies, primarily in the agrarian sector. I had some doubts. I found these ideas quite simplistic. Most of all I wanted to understand how these reforms could be carried out in Latin America and tried to understand more about the history of "policy making" and of "reform mongering" in that part of the world. That is what I have tried to do in my *Journeys Toward Progress*, where for the first time I have written more as a political scientist than as an economist.

You mentioned that President Kennedy had asked you to join his staff and that you refused?
Yes, I had already started writing my book, for which I had just made a lengthy trip through various parts of Latin America that were new to me. Upon my return to New York I was invited to Washington by one of Kennedy's advisers, Richard Goodwin, who was in charge of following the relations with Latin America. We spent a day together in the White House to discuss matters, and he asked me whether I would be interested in joining "Operation Latin America." For various reasons, I decided that I did not want to return to Washington, one reason being that my family and I had reestablished ourselves in New York only two years earlier, after having spent two years at Yale. To move once again would have caused considerable hardship on the family.

But how did you evaluate Kennedy's policy?
I wrote an article about that, in which I criticized American policy with respect to Latin America. The title of the article was "Second Thoughts on the 'Alliance for Progress,'" and I published it in the magazine *The Reporter* directed by Max Ascoli, with whom I had maintained contact over the years. It was a rather harsh critique of Kennedy's simplistic activism with regard to Latin America. The message which I let indirectly transpire was "Leave me alone, please, I just happen not to agree with your policy," but my critique had the opposite effect: it aroused curiosity. The reaction was: Your critique is interesting, explain it at greater length.

In any event, from 1956 on your energies have been primarily devoted to research and teaching?

Until 1968 I continued to work on problems of economic development. My third book on this general theme was the result of a long trip around the world in 1964, 1965, and 1966, to Latin America, but also to parts of Asia and Africa, in the course of which I examined the successes and failures of various development projects that had been financed by the World Bank. This book was entitled *Development Projects Observed*, and I have recently noted that with this book I had hoped to complete a "trilogy" on the general topic of economic development [see chap. 12, "A Hidden Ambition," in *A Propensity to Self-Subversion*]. Actually, I continued being concerned with economic development for a while longer. As I was observing the developing railroads in Nigeria in 1966, I started to write *Exit, Voice, and Loyalty*, which is perhaps my best-known book. Here I deal with more general problems of the social, economic, and political sciences. My interest in this problem may have come from my own life experience, which brought me repeatedly to the question: Should I use exit or voice here?

It seems you took some distance from politics during the sixties. Is this fair to say?

I don't think so. To understand how my ideas on Latin America moved, you should read an article I wrote in Chile in 1967, during a research trip that had taken me primarily to Brazil. That article — which I believe to have been one of my best, or at least one of my most amusing — had the title "Underdevelopment, Obstacles to the Perception of Change, and Leadership." Some people in Chile had really asked me to write something on the "obstacles to development" in Latin America; the idea was widespread then that there are fundamental, "structural" obstacles to change there, such as the agrarian structure. At this point I said to myself: No, I will not write about the obstacles to change, but rather about the obstacles to the *perception* thereof. I had quite a few ideas about that and rapidly wrote the article, which can now be found in my collection *A Bias for Hope: Essays on Development and Latin America.* For the first time, I tried to address myself directly to the Latin American intellectuals and to explain where in my opinion they had gone wrong — that is, how they failed to perceive change. I even coined a term for this type of attitude: "fracasomania," which might be translated as "failure complex." Later I maintained an intensive dialogue with Latin Americans on this matter. I do not know whether this is really a satisfactory reply to your question on my political commitment.

One might say, however, that in your life there has always been this tension or conflict between political militancy, on the one hand, and intellectual work, on the other. In the end, could one say that one of these tendencies has been on the winning side?
No, my life has played itself out like this between two poles. I have never given up looking for new solutions to political problems, and I believe this appears clearly in my recent book *The Rhetoric of Reaction.*

At the present time, you are returning to the problems of the market and of the relations between market and democracy. In this case, your commitment as a scholar is a political commitment. Do you intend to contribute to new solutions in this area?
Yes, to some extent. I have recently written an article, entitled "Reactionary and Progressive Rhetoric," in which there are some new ideas on this theme.

In your long experience as planner, economic expert, and consultant on development, which goes from 1946–47 to the eighties, are there some ideas that remain the same, others that have become transformed in the light of certain experiences?

It is very difficult to answer that question. Perhaps some very general ideas — a certain concept of social justice, the general trust in the democratic idea — have been unchanged by time.

And also a certain propensity for optimism?

Yes, or better, a dislike for too uniform and unilateral diagnoses. I have always had a certain dislike for general principles and abstract prescriptions. I think it is necessary to have an "empirical lantern" or a "visit with the patient" before being able to understand what is wrong with him. It is crucial to understand the peculiarity, the specificity, and also the unusual aspects of the case.

And which of your ideas have changed?

I am in general very attentive to new ideas. I know well that the social world is most variable, in continuous change, that there are no permanent laws. Unexpected events constantly happen, new causality relations are being installed. In that article I mentioned, which goes back to some points of *The Rhetoric of Reaction*, I return to the fact that progressive thought has borrowed some of the typical arguments of rhetoric. In that article I speak at a certain point of a "self-subversive" turn. I have the feeling that this could become a more general theme, because it is possible, even though I have always acted a bit this way, that with age one's new ideas are predominantly those that contradict the old.

Will you therefore subvert yourself?

Self-subversion has been a permanent trait of my intellectual personality. It has often happened to me, in the course of my life, that I have been led to take up the same ideas and reexamine them and find that they lead me on to new angles. This is precisely what happened to me with the "exit/voice" schema. In recent German history there has been a conjunction, even a cooperation of these two elements, exit and voice; while in my original formulation these two were exclusive of one another (the more exit, the less voice, and vice versa). For this reason, my theory was criticized by a German scholar who asserted that the events of Eastern Germany in 1989 contradicted my schema. And this was actually the case! This German situation has given me the opportunity to rethink my discourse and to show why we have not been able to foresee what today can be easily explained; but history was needed to explain the matter to us. By the way, with regard to the problem of economic development, I have had similar moments of self-subversion.

Let us turn for a moment to your relationship with the university. What differences have you found between the American and European academic environments?
You know, I do not have so much experience with university life. I have led a very lonely life in Europe and here too, in America, I have always been quite isolated. In Europe my formation was, as I have said, very chaotic. Two years in Paris, one in London, a year and a half in Trieste. I have never lived with continuity in any university milieu. I should also say that the reactionary climate of the Ecole des Hautes Etudes Commerciales aroused in me feelings close to disgust. Those were the thirties, and in France one also felt at the time a considerable rise of fascism. I have maintained only two friendships from that time, and one certainly cannot say that I lived in an atmosphere that was open and ready for free discussion.

And in the United States?

Here it has been quite different. I was in Berkeley for two years, but during that time I was fully aware of the need to finish my book, knowing that in a short time there would be a new mobilization, so I didn't participate in seminars or campus life. Writing took all my energies. At Yale, later on, I did take part in various seminars, but there, too, I was writing a book with considerable determination. At Columbia University, on the other hand, we had some interesting discussion groups with political scientists like Sam Huntington, Dan Rustow, Daniel Bell, and others. There were good exchanges between us, and I learned a lot from them.

When you were at Columbia, did you continue to frequent the New School for Social Research?

Outside of Columbia, I had few academic contacts in New York. At Harvard, things were altogether different, life in and around seminars was most intensive, perhaps even too much so. There, when people speak in seminars, they think they are making intellectual history, simply because of the fact that they have opened their mouth! In any event I participated in many seminars. I remember that one of the most interesting ones was the one directed by Sam Huntington and Myron Weiner, on economic and political development, which met about once a month.

How did you react to the student movement of 1968?

I was neither as enthusiastic nor as upset as others. For example, Alexander Gerschenkron, who had been a Social Democrat, became a ferocious opponent of the movement. I saw within it some unacceptable forms of behavior, but all in all I saw it as a renewal of social energy, an expression of the will to change. Perhaps the movement was a bit immature, from some points of view. I saw the movement from rather far away, because I spent the crucial year, 1968–69, at the Center for Behavioral Sciences at Stanford. In the chapter on America in *Exit, Voice, and Loyalty* I speak in fact quite positively about the emergence of the Black Power movement as a form of "voice" rather than of "exit." I found myself in the fortunate situation not to have to take a clear position. Otherwise, I would perhaps not have known how to behave.

And what do you think of today's movement in American universities toward "political correctness"?
Here again, there are probably excesses, take for example the position of Professor Jeffreys in New York — not agreeable, on the contrary — but today's use of the expression "political correctness" reminds me of the way the French Left spoke of the Right in France, ridiculing them as "bien pensants." Today, the same attempt is being made: to ridicule a certain left-wing crowd. We speak of "political correctness" in order to ridicule this particular group.

In the seventies and later, history and the history of European thought seem to be again at the center of your attention. In The Passions and the Interests, *for example, you return to some classical themes of political theory. How did you come to this rediscovery after twenty years' experience as an economist of development?*
Perhaps because during this time development itself has experienced tremendous problems. In Latin America (say Brazil, Argentina, Chile), various authoritarian regimes have succeeded each other, and I have come to think that there is a need to understand better the reasons for the birth of democracy and the hopes for its prospects. I have always been interested in the history of ideas, as can be seen even from my first book, *National Power and the*

Structure of Foreign Trade. I am still very impressed by the ideas of Montesquieu and Sir James Steuart, in particular as concerns the connections between politics and economics that were forged in the eighteenth century.

Part Three
Key Terms

Your specific way of posing problems as well as your actual life experiences seem to fall back on a series of central concepts. These concepts, these key terms, can perhaps help us go over, once again, your itinerary. We are thinking specifically of the terms "exit/voice," "trespassing," "bias for hope," "fracasomania," "commitment to doubt," "shifting involvements," and so on. What is the provenance of these ideas? Let's start, with the concept of "unintended consequences," which is so characteristic of your thinking.

In my work I have applied this concept of unexpected consequences a great deal, mainly in connection with the analysis of possible change. I have also taken strong objection to the misuse of the term, which transforms it into a perverse effect and proclaims that any attempt to bring about reform produces exactly the opposite effect. I consider this way of arguing a betrayal of the idea of unintended consequences because it cancels the open-endedness (the open-endedness to a variety of solutions) and substitutes it by total predictability and fear. That is why I call it a betrayal.

But I would like to make a more general observation on these key terms and the way I have tried to utilize them in my work. Take the exit/voice distinction, for example. This distinction has been rather well accepted by the general public and has found many applications. In this respect, you probably know the article by Michael McPherson, which is to be found in the Festschrift published in my honor. McPherson is an economist friend of mine who was the dean of Williams College and was recently appointed president of Macintyre College in St. Paul. In addition to this article in the Festschrift, he also wrote the entry "Hirschman, Albert Otto" in *The New Palgrave: A Dictionary of Economics.*

There McPherson shows that I am pointing to problems that others have not sufficiently considered: if someone proclaims a law, I demonstrate where this law does not function. I believe this is true, but I must say that I also feel the need from time to time to engage in abstract theory. This means that I am not totally "antitheoretical," that I am not totally opposed to parsimony, nor totally in favor of complexity. Some of my ideas are essentially theories of economic development, on the importance of unbalanced growth, for example; the "exit/voice" schema itself may also derive from a new way of looking at social reality.

Similarly, when I wrote my last (or next to last) book, *The Rhetoric of Reaction,* where I subdivided and catalogued various reactionary arguments, I proposed a theoretical argument with categories that did not exist previously. After having read the book, many thought (and this is a curious phenomenon, I think) that these categories had always existed, when instead they are the fruit of my theoretical formulation. The success of a theory consists precisely in that suddenly everyone begins to reason according to the new categories.

Certain concepts appear as if they have existed forever. Such an illusion perhaps results from their ability to speak to common sense. This quality allows certain concepts to assume an aura of timelessness.
Examples of this are the concepts of futility and perversity. The distinction between them had never been pointed out before, at least not to the point where it was shown that there is a clearcut separation and often a contradiction between maintaining that a given policy will not permit you to achieve its assigned objectives, and maintaining that this same policy is entirely in vain. Hence it has been important to point out the difference between these two categories: it had never been done before, even though now one speaks of it as though this distinction had always existed.

In one of the essays in my new book, *A Propensity to Self-Subversion,* I have written that I feel a bit like the mother in that famous Jewish story: The mother gives her son two ties. The son puts one of them on the next day, so as to make the mother happy. The mother then asks him, "So, the other tie, you didn't like it?" In other words, the Jewish mother always administers guilt. I feel I am in a similar position when people praise me for underlining the exceptions to the theories and the rules. Here I am like the Jewish mother of the story. I like to think that I occupy two positions here: I like to underline the exceptions to a theory, but every once in a while I enjoy building up a theory of my own.

The idea of trespassing is basic to my thinking. Even my first book was a book of *sconfinamento,* a book of breaking down barriers. It was a history of the history of ideas. Attempts to confine me to a specific area make me unhappy. When it seems that an idea can be verified in another field, then I am happy to venture in this direction. I believe this is a simple and useful way of discovering "related" topics.

We have already talked about unexpected consequences. I had a great deal of affection for this concept, but then I noted that many people made poor use of it, mainly by using it to bolster reactionary ideas. Hayek, for example, has been most prominent in underlining unexpected effects: he has transformed the concept into a kind of Weltanschauung. In my article about reactionary rhetoric which came out two years after the *Rhetoric of Reaction* [see chap. 2 of *A Propensity to Self-Subversion*]. I refer to Amartya Sen's very fine article on Darwin, where Sen shows that from time to time it is perfectly possible to plan successfully. In other words, we are not always surprised by unexpected consequences.

The concept of "possibilism" occurred to me while I was working on the introduction to my book *A Bias for Hope.* I have always been against the methodology of certain social scientists, and especially of those sociologists who study what has happened in some fifty or so countries and then proceed to draw deductions from there on what is likely to happen in the future. Of course they find themselves without instruments of interpretation in the face of "important exceptions," such as the case of Hitler in Germany. This is the reason I have always disliked certain types of social research. I am always more interested in widening the area of the possible, of what may happen, rather than in prediction, on the basis of statistical reasoning, of what will actually happen. The inquiry into the statistical probability that certain social events will actually take place interests me little; rather, I am interested in finding out whether certain events, good or terrible, are going to take place. I have always found that when something good happens, it occurs as a result of a conjunction of extraordinary circumstances. Somebody who was quite aware of this mechanism was Lenin, even though it squarely contradicted his theoretical declarations according to which revolutionary situations resulted from the convergence of certain objective and subjective conditions. Lenin wrote some particularly interesting passages on how revolutionary circumstances will only come about as a result of extraordinary and unexpected events.

But then how can the social scientist make forecasts?
I simply think that I am not much interested in forecasts; they are not part of my theoretical impulses. There are thinkers who are able to work in this direction — Tocqueville, for example. Daniel Bell is another person who has cultivated this genre. My aim, in any event, is not to forecast tendencies; rather, I am trying to understand what may possibly happen and to shift people's focus

in that direction. Perhaps this is where my activism resurfaces; in this sense I am perhaps still a militant. I always make proposals and try to convince people that certain things are indeed possible. In some of my articles from the 1960s, I proposed the adoption of certain projects with a utopian cast. For example, I suggested that the United States should sell its investments in Latin America and explained in some detail "how to divest." I supported these proposals with a series of technical details that were obviously ridiculous: at that moment nobody was dreaming of setting up such mechanisms. Nonetheless, I still found it interesting at that time to explore the details of the proposal, as though it were possible to actually carry out this policy. I had the impression that in this way the possibility of its adoption would become less remote.

I think that if one is an activist one cannot be a good futurologist: to make effective forecasts, one needs a certain aloofness and even coolness. One has to choose.

One might object to your idea of an opposition between complexity and parsimony by arguing that the social sciences need to be parsimonious since they cannot describe everything. How would you answer?
But I do not propose to include everything. I do try to bring in a few additional concepts, which might make our science more realistic, better. My principal criticism is that the degree of parsimony in economics is too high. Other students of our science, such as Amartya Sen, have sustained similar theses. Sen introduced the concept of "commitment," or "engagement," as a category that determines human experience to a greater extent than rational action. I am talking about categories that are quite important in human experience. When I speak of complexity, I only wish to take into consideration some factors that make the world more complex. but there is no question of opting here between everything and nothing.

And the dyad "passions versus interests"—how has it developed?
Even this antinomy constitutes an extraordinary simplification of human motivation. It is interesting to note how, particularly in the seventeenth and eighteenth centuries, people saw and lived the division between the pursuit of interests, a cold but uninterrupted activity, and the passions, which are on the contrary intrusive, strong, and sudden. With Adam Smith's *Wealth of Nations*, however, this contrast ceases to exist, the passions and the interests come to stand for the same idea and are transformed into a tautology, as I have argued in an article written for the *New Palgrave* entitled, "The Concept of Interest: From Euphemism to Tautology." In the nineteenth century, James Mill observed that people do what they prefer to do, that is, what is in their interest, but as Thomas Babington Macauley wrote, this is hardly a great intuition. The economists followed this line, tending to abstract from psychology, and tried to base their studies on the concept of "revealed preferences," without any attention to psychological motivations, desires, or passions, or their reasonableness.

The idea of "shifting involvements," of oscillation, seems suited to your way of reasoning. Do you mean to say that the desire to find a "point of equilibrium" for one's observations is perhaps misplaced? Isn't it inevitable to change continuously, to oscillate, to modify one's own position?
Most social scientists attempt to establish an optimal degree of government involvement in one sphere or another, for example, the public or the private sphere. But I have often taken the opposite position. In the article I already mentioned where I discuss the possibility of divesting in Latin America, I maintain that in a developing country there may well be an alternation between an "open" phase toward more developed countries, which may then be followed by a restrictive phase when one's own resources and

industries have to be more fully developed. In other words, there are advantages that follow from expanding a good flow of exchanges with foreign countries and others that follow from interrupting such a flow. Thus the idea occurred to me of "shifting involvements," or of oscillation, which I later applied to the involvement of the citizen in public affairs. One can develop a model of alternating phases of opening and closing and demonstrate from the psychological and sociological point of view how this oscillation can be constructive provided its pendulum doesn't swing too far. I expressed this idea for the first time in an international conference in Rio de Janeiro in 1957; I developed it further in *The Strategy of Economic Development*, then in the article on divestment in Latin America, and finally returned to it in my book *Shifting Involvements*, where the idea plays a central role. It can also be found again in *Exit, Voice, and Loyalty*, as an alternation between exit and voice. The recent German applications show that exit and voice, instead of being alternatives, can occur at the same time.

Can this oscillation be described as a regular movement, like that of a pendulum, or is it subject to irregularities?
I would describe it rather as an irregular movement. I am not looking here for a clear and simple idea that would define the term "optimal oscillation." In this respect, I like to quote Blake, who said that to understand what is "enough," we have to know first what is "too much."

The concepts "fracasomania" and "bias for hope" are connected with the idea that one of the most important premises to change is the clear perception of what is already happening by way of change. It is important for people to know that they are already doing something right, that not everything they do is mistaken and must be thrown out — this is an attitude common to many countries, including Italy. The idea occurred to me as a direct result of my studies of policy making in Latin America, but is also due to my Italian experience. While I was writing, my ears were ringing with certain phrases that one cannot avoid hearing in Italy, such as "Povera Italia!" The idea of "fracasomania," or failure complex, also occurred to me as a result of my observation of Colombia and Brazil. In Colombia, the land reform that had been promoted in the thirties by the New Dealish government of Alfonso López, had always been interpreted as a total failure; but the data I had been able to collect indicated some changes in a positive direction. In Brazil, there had been similar attempts at land reform in the northeast of the country, which in many ways resembles the Italian Mezzogiorno. Here the public works that were supposed to fight the drought led only to corruption and the waste of a great deal of money. It seemed that everything had failed, that despite all the effort nothing had succeeded. And yet, as I watched more closely, I found that something had worked out. Thus I elaborated the concept of "fracasomania" and, by antithesis, the idea of a "bias for hope," of a prejudice in favor of hope, which goes along with the idea of change.

Is "fracasomania" a synonym of "catastrophism"?
No, catastrophism is rather an either/or analysis, such as the reasoning that either you carry out this reform or there will be a catastrophe — a very different set of ideas.

Is "fracasomania" a term that might be applied to what happens now in the eastern European countries?
Perhaps, to some extent. The theme can be said to be related to the theory of dependency. In Latin America young people were sent to study in the United States or at European universities,

and when they return they are convinced they know everything and have nothing to learn from the older generation that has always lived in Latin America. The result is an absence of contact and interchange between young and old generations. This is another form of "fracasomania."

How do you see the relation between change and progress? Is it still possible to use the term "progress"?
To use a term that is so discredited, you mean? As long as I am still primarily an economist, I believe there is still a way of measuring economic performances and therefore of speaking of measurable progress. For example, there is no doubt that Latin America has made considerable progress in the thirty years since World War II, that it has taken part in *les trente glorieuses*. But this has been said and recognized only in the eighties, in a period, that is, when the economy had gone into decline. Before that, the Latin American intellectuals were never ready to admit, throughout that thirty-year period, that their countries were passing through an ascending phase. They were only ready to do so in the eighties, when they could claim that things were in a dreadful state. This sort of thing happens often in Europe. When did Fourastié actually coin the expression "les trente glorieuses"? When those "glorious" years were safely over! In this connection it is interesting to note that social and economic progress do not always go together. Infant mortality may substantially decline and literacy can rise, that is, the "social indicators" can show improvement while economic indexes are stationary or are even going down. One reason for such unexpected behavior is that at one point mothers may learn new ways, such as how to boil water and how to send the children to school, regardless of actual income. I have written about this under the title "The On-and-Off Connection Between Political and Economic Progress."

Another original and persistent characteristic of your reflections seems to be your "trust in doubt," even what might be considered a true profession of faith in doubt.

You have, in fact, identified an important aspect of my thinking. I thought about it in particular when I wrote my talk for the honorary doctorate from the University of Turin in 1987. I wanted to write something about what I had learned from my brother-in-law Eugenio Colorni. This is one of the things I most appreciated about him: his search for truth and his systematic doubt. As his ingenious mind passed from one idea to another, so it went from one doubt to the next. The two things were not simultaneous, but they were closely connected. Every new intuition was accompanied by a new doubt. It ended up an interesting and most pleasurable activity. Ideas and doubts were inseparable.

Let's go back to your concept of self-subversion. Is it in some way related to that of trespassing?

Actually, they are both tied to my desire to rehabilitate words that have somehow assumed a negative meaning. I have done so with the expression "a bias for hope." In English, "bias" definitely has a negative connotation; it means prejudice, whereas by connecting it with "hope" I have given it a positive connotation. Also "trespassing" is often used in a negative sense in our country — for example, in those public posters where the inscription "No trespassing!" warns against some imagined violation of private property rights. But, the way I use it, the term assumes once again a positive value: the injunction to trespass means passing beyond the disciplinary boundaries or passing from one discipline to another without rigidity. (The authors of my Festschrift went back to this idea, incorporating it into the book's title, which was *Development, Democracy, and the Art of Trespassing*.) A similar change in standard usage is meant to take place with the

term "subversion," which normally carries a negative connotation. Now you are writing about "subversion" or "self-subversion"? What a terrible thing!

*Are there any other key words we should add to those we have already
discussed ?*
It may be helpful to move from key words to *play* words, or, better, to "play on words." I enjoy playing with words, inventing
new expressions. I believe there is much more wisdom in words
than we normally assume. It frequently happens to me that I find
confirmation of an intuition in a literary passage or a poem. Here
is an example. One of my recent antagonists, Mancur Olson,
uses the expression "logic of collective action" in order to demonstrate the illogic of collective action, that is, the virtual unlike-
lihood that collective action can ever happen. At some point, I
was thinking about the fundamental rights enumerated in the
Declaration of Independence and that beautiful expression of
American freedom as "the right to life, liberty, and the pursuit
of happiness." I noted how, in addition to the pursuit of happiness, one might also underline the importance of the *happiness
of pursuit,* which is precisely the felicity of taking part in collective action. I simply was happy when that play on words occurred
to me.

Here is another example of this kind of play on words. In the
article on how to divest in Latin America, I talked about the role
of foreign capital, which is usually considered to be very powerful. But the opposite may happen: the foreign investor may never
feel part of the political life of the country and remain marginal
to it, in part because he is a foreigner, in part because he is an
immigrant. Hence, the problem with foreign capital, I said, may
not be so much that the foreign capitalist is too meddlesome, but
that he is too "mousy"! This particular play on words (meddle-

some, mousy) may not be particularly funny, yet it carries with it an unusual association that is easily remembered.

Here's an indication of just how important and inspiring language is to me. Over the years I have gradually compiled a series of quotes from readings of my favorite authors — Montaigne, Pascal, Flaubert, and so on. I gave this list to my daughter Lisa on the day of her graduation from college, a list that I continue to update.

Among these quotes I remember in particular a marvelous sentence from the Marquise de Merteuil in *Dangerous Liaisons*: "On acquiert rarement les qualités dont on peut se passer" (One rarely acquires the qualities one can do without), which I used to good effect in my article "Obstacles to Development." Similarly, in my essay on the tension between morality and the social sciences, I have been inspired by the lines of a short poem by Hölderlin: "Hast du Verstand und ein Herz, so zeige nur eines von beiden, Beides verdammen Sie dir, zeigest Du beides zugleich" (If you have brains and a heart, show only one or the other, for you will get credit for neither should you show both at once"). At the heart of my article is the idea of an inevitable tension between morality and social knowledge. Some of these poetical expressions are like stations where I may take a rest during my work and which help me to push on. Perhaps this is another attempt of mine at trespassing, this time from the social sciences to literature.

In a recent article on social conflict I quote another sentence of Hölderlin, which is famous as well as quite beautiful: "Wo aber Gefahr ist, wächst das rettende auch" (Where there is danger, there is also deliverance). Here Hölderlin almost seems to suggest that the greater the risk, the greater the hopes for salvation — something that surely is not invariably true. It's a beautiful thought, perhaps combined with a certain amount of folly — a significant fact in the case of Hölderlin.

It is interesting anyway to introduce poetry into the discourse here. When it so happens that I find an expression like the "happiness of pursuit" instead of the "pursuit of happiness," I feel I have the right to push further along that line of thought to its end. I believe to have caught something real.

At a certain point in my life, I even cultivated an interest in palindromes. I have invented a few and made a collection, in various languages, which I gave to my other daughter, Katia, for her graduation. In the palindrome tradition, I entitled this collection *Senile Lines* and signed it "Dr. Awkward." One of those I was most proud of (because I don't think it has ever been discovered by anyone else) is "Miasma is Siam's aim" (which is wrong, since Siam was one of those economic miracle countries; but, anyway, it's a good palindrome). To play with words in this way is an amusing pastime, but when I make these kinds of inventions I feel a push to venture farther along, I feel that it may be worthwhile to explore the matter more thoroughly. Like when I find an opposition between the words "meddlesome" and "mousy," I suspect that I may have caught something "real," a much-needed confirmation in the solitude of writing. It may seem strange, but all these linguistic inventions are, much like quotes from poetry, instruments of support: they make me feel safer and stronger, when I follow up some thought process.

Your activity as a social scientist seems to be based on the idea of using reason for the purpose of discovering things that are to be found at a more hidden level. To do this one must be quite imaginative, and one can hardly be satisfied with a flat description of reality. What relation exists between this exercise of fantasy and creativity, on the one hand, and, on the other, the activity of describing in scientific terms what has been elaborated by those means?
I believe that we must accept a bit of oscillation in our own work

too! In other words, when working, there are sometimes moments of poetic enthusiasm, and other times moments of rational ordering and cataloguing. I often have the experience of rewriting a text completely or in part. Sometimes I have the sensation of being involved with a text that I am not yet capable of disentangling. This is not an easy activity to talk about, but I believe I have found a degree of security and pleasure in connecting my *thinking* process with linguistic invention and the ideas of the great thinkers. This *conjunction* is a remarkable event that gives me new strength to go forward.

It does not seem to me that you are following very closely Hölderlin's advice to reveal either brains or heart, but not both at the same time. In your analyses they always go together.
That is true. In fact, in one of my articles I express the hope that my grandchildren will be able to enjoy a social science where the disjunction of brains and heart is not a must, so that they would not have to live by the Hölderlin rule. I hope that the two will somehow meet.

At one point you asserted that if we were ever to achieve total success in the social sciences, we should be prepared to experience the total failure of the human being.
Yes, this idea came to me at the end of a conversation with the Swedish sociologist Richard Swedberg. I had said something of the kind, using perhaps a milder tone, in the preface to *A Bias for Hope.* As I said there, if we had the ability to foretell the future, or if we found ourselves facing a totally applicable sociological law, we would then be the first ones to feel frustrated and disappointed. In other words, I like to combine the pleasure of theory building with that of theory smashing. This is the reason why I usually introduce, in the first part of my writings, some schema

which is then exposed to critiques, pointing out its limitations, in the second part. Perhaps the best example of this tendency of mine is contained in an article, written around 1970, on the tolerance of inequality in the process of economic development. There I introduce the concept of the "tunnel effect," a theoretical invention that has had a remarkable resonance. (When one invents a theoretical concept, a common reaction is the exclamation "How come I didn't think of that beforehand?")

The "tunnel effect" may occur when my economic position not only doesn't improve in relation to someone else's, but instead the other person experiences the financial improvement I had expected for myself. Instead of being envious, I may be hopeful that my turn to experience improvement will come in due course. The tunnel effect will take place only under certain circumstances, which I explore in the second part of the article. Thus I begin my article with a strong statement (the tunnel effect exists) which is then immediately restricted by various limitations on the margins of validity of my schema. This is the pattern I like to follow in the process of evolving a theory. I have acted similarly with respect to my "exit/voice" theory, but perhaps not strongly enough: for quite a few years after my original formulation, I have come across situations where exit and voice do not act in opposition to each other, but rather work in conjunction. This is a good example for my argument "against parsimony," or, to be more exact, in favor of more complexity. Yet these two aspects could not be expressed at the same time if one did not initially restrict the field of speculation. This observation takes us back to the key word we noted earlier, that is, "oscillation."

In our conversation we have talked a bit about your masters and teachers, but less about your enemies. Who are they? Who have they been over the years and what were the ideas you felt most impelled to fight and argue against?

True, one often writes against someone, even if unconsciously. I already mentioned Mancur Olson and his well-known book *The Logic of Collective Action,* which is based on the idea that the rational actor is a "free rider," someone who does not take part in collective action, counting on others to do it in his stead, so that "collective action" will rarely take place. Instead, I have spent several years arguing, particularly to economists, that collective action does exist and that people do take part in it. And in the end I came up with a formulation that is part of my argument against parsimony. Once again I refer to a phrase by Pascal that I found particularly striking: "The hope Christians have to possess an infinite good is mixed with actual enjoyment...for they are not like those people who would hope for a kingdom in which they, as subjects, have no stake; rather, they hope for holiness, and for freedom from injustice, and they partake of both."

Speaking of enemies, I have had quite a few, especially in the years I worked on the problem of development. Initially, as I explained in my article "A Dissenter's Confession," I was a member of a group of new theorists of economic development within which I represented the role of the dissenter; nevertheless, I was considered part of the group. We were united by certain common characteristics, such as the automatic application of orthodox remedies to the problems of development: all one needs to do is to let things proceed "naturally" and everything will proceed well. Some common characteristics united these people, and they were then called "high development theorists." In an interesting interview, Paul Krugman, a young MIT economist, said that certain writers, such as Arthur Lewis, Paul Rosenstein-

Rodan, Gunnar Myrdal, and Albert Hirschman, should be "rehabilitated" as a group who made important contributions to economic development in the fifties. Now it is true that all of us had something in common, because we all recognized that the "underdeveloped" countries, as they were called then, needed to adopt certain public policies. Yet there was a considerable difference between my theories and those of the other members of the group. When I wrote *The Strategy of Economic Development,* my "enemies" were exactly those people with whom my name is now being associated. I had written largely against the theory of balanced growth proposed by Rosenstein-Rodan and by Ragnar Nurkse. In my book there is a whole chapter, quite sarcastic, entitled "Balanced Growth: A Critique," followed by another important chapter that is entitled "Unbalanced Growth: An Espousal." This just goes to show that one often has *intimate* enemies and to tell who they were.

Let me say a word about *Exit, Voice, and Loyalty.* This book is largely written against those who talk about competition as the solution to every problem. According to this vision, exit, or the passing to a competitive alternative, is the ideal corrector of monopolistic situations. My argument was rather that an important corrective role can often be played by voice just as much as by exit.

In my first book, *National Power and the Structure of Foreign Trade,* the enemy was a certain orthodoxy. If you read my last book, *The Rhetoric of Reaction,* it is not hard to figure out who my enemy is. Maybe other books have "enemies" that are more difficult to isolate and identify. Until you just asked me, I had never thought about my books in that way — as attacks on certain enemies.

Perhaps your greatest enemy is still orthodoxy.

Certainly, orthodoxy, even though I have often tried to maintain contact with orthodox economists. (In this sense I feel different from John Kenneth Galbraith and other nonorthodox economists, since I try to keep in contact with people from other camps.) So, in the end, you are right. The principal enemy is orthodoxy: to use the same recipe, administer the same therapy, to resolve the most various types of problems; never to admit complexity and try to reduce it as much as possible, while ignoring that things are always more complicated in reality.

Before we finish up here, I would like to mention my favorite book, *The Passions and the Interests*. This has been a very important book for me. It really was the fruit of free creation. I did not write it against anybody. To me it represents the free discovery of connections between various ideas. That book gave me prolonged pleasure: to write, feeling free to discover things without having to prove someone wrong. A very special case, and one that the Princeton University Press recently reprinted in a new twentieth-anniversary edition.

Translated from the Italian and edited by Albert O. Hirschman.

Bibliography

BOOKS

National Power and the Structure of Foreign Trade. Berkeley: University of California Press, 1945. Reprinted 1969; expanded paperback edition with new introduction, 1980.

The Strategy of Economic Development. New Haven: Yale University Press, 1958. Reprinted 1978 by the Norton Library; in 1988 by Westview Press.

Journeys Toward Progress: Studies of Economic Policy-Making in Latin America. New York: Twentieth Century Fund, 1963. Reprinted 1973 by The Norton Library with a new preface.

Development Projects Observed. Washington, DC: Brookings Institution, 1967. Re-edited, with a new preface by the author, the Brookings Institution, 1995.

Exit, Voice, and Loyalty: Responses to Decline in Firms, Organizations, and States. Cambridge: Harvard University Press, 1970.

The Passions and the Interests: Political Arguments for Capitalism Before Its Triumph. Princeton: Princeton University Press, 1977. Twentieth Anniversary Edition, 1997, by Princeton University Press, with a foreword by Amartya Sen and a second preface by the author.

Shifting Involvements: Private Interest and Public Action. Princeton: Princeton University Press, 1982.

Getting Ahead Collectively: Grassroots Experiences in Latin America. Photographs by Mitchell Denbury. Pergamon Press, 1984.

The Rhetoric of Reaction: Perversity, Futility, Jeopardy. Cambridge: Belknap Press, 1991.

Crossing Boundaries: Selected Writings. New York: Zone Books, 1998.

COLLECTIONS OF ESSAYS

A Bias for Hope: Essays on Development and Latin America. New Haven: Yale University Press, 1971 (16 essays). Reprinted 1985 by Westview Press.

Essays in Trespassing: Economics to Politics and Beyond. Cambridge, UK: Cambridge University Press, 1981 (14 essays).

Rival Views of Market Society and Other Recent Essays. London: Viking/Penguin, 1986 (10 essays). Paperback edition, with new preface by the author, Harvard University Press, 1992.

A Propensity to Self-Subversion. Cambridge: Harvard University Press, 1995 (20 essays).

Designed by Bruce Mau with Barr Gilmore
Typeset by Archetype
Printed and casebound by Maple-Vail on Sebago acid-free paper